99 Habit Success Stories

Michal Stawicki & Jeannie Ingraham

99 HABIT SUCCESS STORIES

TABLE OF CONTENTS

"We are what we repeatedly do. Excellence, then, is not an act, but a habit."

— Will Durant

How Push-ups and Emailing Tina Fey Produced This Book

From Michal:

Around April 2006, I stepped onto the scale. It read over 158 pounds. The figure on the scale was definitely too high for a 5′5″ guy. I never liked to exercise, and as an IT specialist I led a sedentary lifestyle. My weight had been climbing for the last few years since I graduated from university and got a full-time job sitting behind a desk. I needed to do something about this.

I decided to do a series of push-ups every day. In the past, I had maintained this discipline for months or even years at a time. However, the idea that I could outwork a crappy diet was ridiculous. Especially with only a single series of bodyweight exercises per day. I kept gaining weight for the next few years.

But I also kept my push-up habit. And it changed my life.

Let's go back to April 2006. You already know that I was overweight.

I also had a job that I moderately liked. It wasn't a great gig to be passionate about, but it put food on the table.

However, we still struggled financially. Luckily, we had no major unexpected expenses. But keeping 2–3% of my salary at the end of the month was a struggle. And whenever any major expense materialized, it wiped out our savings account to the last dime. A few months after I restarted my push-up habit, we bought a small flat. Our mortgage was more than 100% of the flat's value. We spent our savings on bank and tax fees. The last dimes went to purchasing a bed for our two sons. We needed to wait for my next paycheck to buy more furniture.

Money was always a problem.

I was also closed-minded and shy. I never spoke with strangers. I was happy to be confined to the social bubble of my immediate family, workmates, and church community.

Financial problems strained our marriage. My wife wanted a better lifestyle, but how the heck was I supposed to provide it? I changed jobs. The salary was much better, but the commute was almost twice as long and I spent less time at home. My wife waited till our third child reached preschool age, and then she found a job too.

I was moderately depressed. I didn't see the sense in my life. I worked around the clock only to spend everything in the next month. Work, home, work, home, work... A typical Western hamster wheel.

My push-up habit saved my life.

Fast forward to December 2019:

- I have a different job. It pays better per hour, and I work only 10 hours a week there. I started a few side-hustle careers — author, coach, and book marketer — and they put bread on the table plus some.

- My health is terrific. I can do more than 160 pushups in one session. To be exact, 166 is my record. I've been sick only three times since July 2013.

- We have over 16,000 dollars sitting in a savings account, and it's only because we spent 11,000 dollars this year on a house renovation, a new car, two trips to the States, and some other flamboyancies.

- My income has almost tripled since 2006. I have written

and published 16 books. Some of them were translated into German, Spanish, and Chinese. I also coach one-on-one online and advertise other authors' books.

- I've developed plenty of new skills, like advertising books on Amazon, building a following on social media, and managing a blog. Did I mention that I've written over 2 million words and my answers on Quora.com have been viewed 8 million times?

- My spiritual life has boomed. I pray as much as I've ever prayed in my life. I study Scripture and the writings of saints on an everyday basis. I definitely see the purpose in my life.

- I overcame my shyness. In fact, I have dozens of new friends all over the world.

- My wife quit her job in 2017, and we are slowly working on getting our relationship back on track.

- I changed my mindset about success and life in general. I look forward to the future with anticipation.

And all of that happened because I decided to start my push-up habit in 2006. Can you connect the dots between a single small habit and such a massive life transformation? I can. It's easy when you look back.

However, when you look ahead, it's close to impossible. You can only see obstacles and struggles. And you have no idea how a small, simple habit like doing a series of push-ups can help you to deal with this overwhelming stuff. The math just doesn't work, right? One small habit. A whole life turned around. What the heck?

My story is not an aberration. When scientists tried to determine the real cause behind life-transformation stories, they looked for significant events: life's drama, accidents, death in the family, winning the lottery, starting a family, and divorces. To their amazement, they discovered that in most cases the thing that started the whole process of a life change was a habit.

You need good habits in life to succeed. Unfortunately, obstacles and difficulties dim your vision. You cannot connect the dots between a habit and success in advance.

That's why Jeannie and I decided to write this book. We provide 99 stories connecting the dots backward. All of the stories are true. They happened in the lives of people like you and me — women, men, living on all the continents and speaking in various languages.

Read those stories and believe in the life-transforming power of habits. Get the determination to start a new habit. Well started is half-done. All you need to do afterward is keep going.

You will succeed.

From Jeannie:

When I first met Michal — electronically — a few years ago, it was nothing but a fluke. As a writer, I had learned that I liked validation for my writing, and I thought other writers would like the same. Turns out it's true. So, whenever I read a book that speaks to me, I email the writer and thank them for writing the book. Most of the time, they write me back, grateful for my short, personal email.

I'm not just talking about self-published writers like me and Michal, but big names. Neil Gaiman, Rainbow Rowell, and Charles Duhigg, for starters. And yes, I get responses. My favorite response is from Tina Fey:

From Jeannie: *I just loved your book. Thanks for representing us funny, writerly, mom bosses!*

From Tina: *I've got spaghetti in my hair. It's been there since yesterday.*

It was all the validation I needed to continue the habit.

To pay the bills—because starving artist, right?—I had been ghostwriting, quite prolifically for a couple of years, when a new client sent me one of Michal's books as an example of what he wanted. I had never heard of him before, but the cover was pleasing, and I had to read it to get an idea of what the client wanted. I typically hate the hyped-up, vapid self-help that I so often had to write for others (You thought they all wrote their own? Nope. Michal is a bit of an oddity!), but I hated reading it even more. I was pleasantly surprised by Michal's book, and his authenticity. I told my client that I just couldn't write a book for him like this because Michal's cornerstone characteristic was his raw authenticity, and you just can't get that with a "rah, rah, go get them, platform-building book" that was ghostwritten.

But, like all writers whose book I enjoyed, I sent Michal an email. I had no idea he was self-published. Or that he was a mild-mannered Polish IT guy.

He emailed me back and asked if I could help him with a project he had been working on but was struggling with. And so I took his notes, and the stories he had gathered, and thus was born *99 Perseverance Success Stories*, which has been one of our bestselling books. Still is.

Eventually, Michal approached me about writing a second in the series. We threw around a couple of ideas.

Previously we had talked specifically about perseverance leading to success, but I realized that many times it was habits that had allowed these people to persevere.

And since it was my idiosyncratic habit of thanking authors that brought us together, we decided we would write about habits. Both Michal and I are habit junkies. The small habits that we had both worked on had an effect like compound interest.

Most of the habits you'll encounter in this book are small, daily habits that have a compounding effect. There are, however, times when change happens all at once. Something big happens that changes the way we see or do everything. However, it's not the big event that leads to the change. Many times, these changes lead to some kind of keystone habit, which Michal already touched on.

For me, my big keystone habit change was brought on suddenly with my being diagnosed with celiac disease in 2016, a year of great change for me and for Michal. Celiac is that pesky autoimmune disease that forces on you a strict gluten-free diet. No cheating, ever. And it wasn't the kind of gluten free that is quite a fad now, or like those who have a sensitivity or an allergy. I could no longer eat out. I had to wash and sort all my grains, legumes, fruits, and veggies to ensure no gluten had entered my house. I had to cook all my food from scratch. I quickly learned that gluten-free labeling in the USA was basically useless for me. Gluten exposure is measured in PPM, parts per million, and in the USA, anything less than 20 PPM gluten is considered gluten free. However, anything more than 0 PPM makes me violently sick. Sorry, those Cheerios will still kill me.

Like I was, my mother was also diagnosed with celiac,

only a few years earlier, and for her it was too late. As she lost her pancreas and became a type-3 diabetic, as her spleen failed, as her appendix ruptured and her gallbladder was removed, I saw the results of keeping any amount of gluten in my life. I like my organs right where they are.

My beauty products, household supplies—even the envelopes I use—had to be changed. I couldn't even smoke cigarettes because they use gluten in the glue that holds the paper in a cylinder. With the short phrase, "Your results for celiac are positive," my whole life changed. I was forced into dozens of new habits daily. I saw that even though I did better than average with my habits, I had so many bad habits that I didn't even see.

That's the power of habits, both good and bad. They work in the background, forming who we are now.

I could no longer run through McDonald's and grab a cheeseburger if I was out running errands and got hungry. If I forgot my new snacks of fruit or nuts, I had to wait till I got home. I couldn't just throw my produce from grocery shopping in the fridge to forget about it; I would have to carefully wash and inspect everything before I put it away, which led to chopping and meal prepping. And a weight loss of 60 pounds in a year. In 2016 I weighed almost 270 pounds, and as of today in 2019, I'm down to 190. And still going.

I'm beginning to see the massively compounding interest of most of these habits only now, even though my life changed drastically within a few days. It was hard at first. Now, I think nothing of reading labels before I buy anything. Or prepping my meals. Or washing my food, and then cleaning my kitchen while I'm at it. My friends know not to invite me out for lunch (there's this place in my town where the owner is a celiac, and I sometimes eat there), but instead come over for me to cook, or go for a hike, which has increased my hospitality habit—more on that later—and my exercise habit.

Even if you have a drastic change in your life, something big that changes everything, it takes a while to see the benefit of those. And sometimes, it takes a bit to see the full benefit from that massive change.

And that's why perseverance and habits go hand in hand toward leading us to success. You can't have one without the other. If you fail to persevere, then the habits will fail. And if you never make a habit, you don't build your perseverance tolerance. If you don't build habits, there's nothing to persevere over.

Michal and I hope you enjoy our latest book, and that in it, you will be able to find some habits that will help you develop your own success. Some habits contradict each other: Some experts suggest getting off social media, while others claim some kind of social-media habit is the key to their success. Some may not work for your situation: If you work in a corporate setting, perhaps a two-hour nap in the afternoon is off the docket. Some are little incremental changes, while others are wildly ambitious.

But we're sure there's a keystone habit in these pages that will speak to you and help you develop a more productive, successful life.

Michal and Jeannie

LUDVIG SUNSTROM

Ludvig started meditating several years ago and saw some great results. Then about a year-and-a-half later, he added power napping into his daily schedule, for around ten minutes at a time, sometimes multiple times a day. After this he noticed a big difference in his life, which manifested itself in two ways:

- He was able to work in spurts with intense focus, which was followed up by a period of rest and recuperation, making him able to repeat the cycle.

- He was able to keep his focus more consistently throughout the day.

Meditation helped Ludvig to ignore the unnecessary and irrelevant things in his life so that he could better focus on the task at hand. For the last six months or so, he's also begun writing down his "daily lessons" every night. This takes less than ten minutes (usually around five minutes), but he finds it extremely helpful. It's a good habit because it forces him to think about what he's learned every day. He firmly believes that if you're able to accumulate many of these small positive habits, then they'll all add up to big things! Just taking a few minutes out of his day to practice these habits has made Ludvig more productive, focused, rested, and therefore successful.

Ludvig is a popular podcast host, bestselling author, and blogger. You can find out more about him at
http://ludvigsunstrom.com/

TIMO KIANDER

The small habit that Timo has found heavily impacts his life is that of setting a task limit. Every night before going to sleep, he completes a list of tasks that he wants to accomplish the next day. This takes around twenty minutes or so, but it's well worth it. The act of formulating and setting out goals for tomorrow is not only relaxing (which means he sleeps better and is better rested), but also makes him more productive.

He has seen a dramatic effect when it comes to productivity in his life since he began this habit, and the difference between now and his previous "non-task-list" life really surprises him. And he finds that if for some reason he fails to write a task list in the evening, he goes to bed feeling helpless and lost, and sleeping is very difficult. Putting all those tasks on paper, knowing that he won't forget anything and that he has a plan to get things done, makes Timo rest easy at night. And, of course, it makes the next day's work a lot easier. Timo thinks this is proof of how deeply engrained this habit is that nowadays he just can't sleep without writing out that task list!

To learn more about Timo, visit his website:
http://www.productivesuperdad.com/

STEVE SCOTT

For a long time, Scott was struggling with certain aspects of productivity. More specifically, he'd always end up starting each day by "putting out fires" (dealing with emergency issues and issuing first aid, rather than solving long-term problems) and responding to the demands of other people. That meant that by the time he got to the afternoon, both his energy and his motivation would be at almost zero. Scott found he really wasn't at his best when he needed to work on important projects of his own.

But then he started a habit that has really had an impact on how he works and spends his time. Every morning he spends five minutes identifying the three tasks for the day that are going to have the biggest influence on his life or his business. Then he works on those three items before he does anything else at all.

This habit brings success because it forces you to make clear choices about which tasks are truly important and which can be saved for later, thus helping you work on projects when you're at your best and have peak energy levels.

Scott is a successful businessman with a solid five-figure monthly income, showing that discipline can lead to extraordinary results! To learn more about Scott, visit his website:

https://www.developgoodhabits.com/

LIDIYA K

Lidiya's habit is maybe a bit surprising, but it's something that she's truly found both helps and inspires her. She believes that reading is a very powerful habit. You might roll your eyes at that, but Lidiya honestly thinks that the ability to read (and the discipline to sit down and do it) is one of the greatest things she acquired in childhood. Reading for even as little as ten minutes per day can inspire you, help you grow, bring the seeds of new ideas, and even expand your consciousness, depending on the text that you choose to spend time with.

She sets aside at least ten minutes a day to read. It doesn't particularly matter when this ten-minute period happens, though she has noticed that making it a part of her morning or evening routine gives her the best results, so you might want to start with that. During this period she simply reads—nothing else—usually motivational literature, philosophy, or something otherwise inspiring.

Lidiya says that this little habit does work wonders, particularly if you're some kind of writer, though anyone can benefit from the habit of reading. Lidiya has made quite the journey in her life, starting with nothing and building a blogging empire, which has allowed her to travel and live all over the world, including in Amsterdam.

Lidiya's habit has certainly propelled her to success; check out her successful blog:

https://letsreachsuccess.com/

CRYSTAL

As Crystal was trying to think of a ten-minute success story that she'd experienced, the first thing that sprang to mind was her Scripture study. A few years ago she had a hard time even bringing herself to open the Scriptures, but she started with just one or two minutes of reading per day. Over time, reading became easier and she eventually increased her time to ten to fifteen minutes. Now she's grown to love reading the Scriptures.

Applying the ten-minute philosophy here didn't just help Crystal create a good habit, but it also helped bring her closer to God. Those ten minutes of calm and contemplation in her day really have an effect. If she ever gets too busy and forgets to read, even just for one day, she feels a difference. She says she doesn't feel as peaceful, as calm, or as loving. Crystal guesses that this is the whole reason for establishing good habits — we gain a lot of benefit if we are consistent in practicing every day.

The great thing is that we start with baby steps; just ten minutes per day has such a big impact on your life. Nowadays, Crystal couldn't imagine being without the calm and peace that her ten minutes of Scripture-reading per day brings her. And of course, she brings that calm and peace into everything else that she faces during the day.

Skye Mooney

Skye has actually made several progressive, small changes that have become habits that have changed her life.

It all began when she was retaining water. Skye had always struggled to make herself drink properly, so she decided that she would start every day with a 600ml bottle of water (about two glasses). It didn't take long for this to easily become a habit. And it meant that she started out her day hydrated, which encouraged her to stay hydrated throughout the day because she knew how good it felt.

She then moved on to the extra vegetables that she knew she really needed to add to her diet. Working on the same principle, she decided to start eating veggies at breakfast time. It was a bit strange at first, but it wasn't especially difficult. This soon became a habit that added at least two to three extra servings of vegetables to her diet. As an added bonus, this also meant that the amount of refined carbs (breads and cereals, specifically) that she was eating decreased.

Over time Skye made many more small and easy changes: swapping seed oils for coconut oils, for example, or regular grains for whole grains. By instituting these habits one at a time, she found making the changes to be easy. It hardly took any time from her day. And by doing this consistently over the last year, Skye has completely changed her lifestyle and lost thirteen kilos, or 29 pounds, as well!

Pyotr Ilyich Tchaikovsky

Tchaikovsky is famous for his sweeping orchestral music, such as the *1812 Overture*, as well as his complex piano pieces. But this Romantic composer also suffered from depression, as well as undergoing many personal crises throughout his lifetime.

He did have a very specific habit that he believed led to his musical success, however. Every day, without exception, Tchaikovsky would walk for exactly two hours. Where he walked didn't matter, and he would wander through woods or cities, wherever he happened to be. What did matter was the duration. It had to be two hours, not a minute more, nor a minute less. He was certain that deviating by even one minute would lead to mishap or misfortune.

Tchaikovsky's habit may be a little unusual, and even compulsion. But it's undebatable that he was one of the premiere composers and musicians of his day. His success is still familiar to most of us, and his music is played by some of the largest and most famous orchestras in the world. Habits such as exercise are known to help alleviate symptoms of depression. So if you find yourself blue, or even suffer from clinical depression like Tchaikovsky, going for a walk, run, or hitting the gym will help you kick depression to the curb.

For more reading on Tchaikovsky, you can visit the Kennedy Center for the Arts:

https://www.kennedy-center.org/artist/C3651

LUDWIG VAN BEETHOVEN

Beethoven's work is some of the most famous and recognizable classical music in the world. From Japan to his native Germany, the *Moonlight Sonata*, his piano sonatas, and his orchestral symphonies are played by students and professionals. His Ninth Symphony is even used as the anthem of the European Union.

Despite a life plagued with difficulties, including falling in love with a woman far outside his rank, as well as becoming completely deaf by the end of his life, Beethoven was one of the most popular composers and pianists of his time. The habit that he thought ensured his success? He drank around fifty cups of tea per day!

Of course, we can't exactly say that tea wrote the *Moonlight Sonata*, but without it, who knows? Beethoven's musical genius is indisputable, and his compositions continue to inspire awe to this day. In line with his compulsive tea-drinking, doctors and medical professionals recommend, depending on your weight, drinking about 64oz of water per day because it leads to better skin, digestion, and cognition. Maybe Beethoven was on to something with his tea even though doctors of his time weren't aware of the benefits of hydration.

For further reading on Beethoven, visit the American Beethoven Society online:

https://americanbeethovensociety.org

INGMAR BERGMAN

Swedish film director Ingmar Bergman is considered one of the most influential filmmakers of modern times. Responsible for such movies as *Fanny and Alexander, Wild Strawberries,* and *Scenes from a Marriage,* Bergman directed over sixty films, and was also a prolific theatre director. His works are renowned for being dark, often dealing with the themes of death and infidelity.

Bergman lived a difficult life. He hated school and was often accused of being obsessive about his work. Despite his hardships, he still managed to produce some of the greatest films of the twentieth century.

His habits for success were quite unique. Bergman refused to drink alcohol, and he never took any medicines. It is important to note that many medicines of his day are now considered illegal drugs. While it seems many creatives imbibe too often, Bergman believed he needed to be fully present. Today, many other successful people follow this example, which can be seen in the proliferation of places like dry bars. Being fully present and in control, he was able to be extremely disciplined with his many daily rituals. For example, he ate exactly the same lunch every day — another simplifying habit, like wearing a professional uniform, that many modern busy celebrities, such as Barack Obama, share.

Building the habit of discipline almost certainly allowed Bergman to work as much as he did, so perhaps we should be thankful that Bergman chose to eat cottage cheese and strawberry jam every lunchtime!

To learn more about the director, visit the Austin Film Society's celebration for his centennial:

https://www.austinfilm.org/series/ingmar-bergmans-centennial/

FRIEDRICH SCHILLER

Eighteenth-century German Friedrich Schiller was a man of many professions. Most notably, Schiller was a poet, though he was also a philosopher, historian, playwright, and a physician. Schiller is one of the most famous and respected members of Germany's literary elite to this day, and was close friends with Goethe, another leading German writer.

Though Schiller's family was often poor (his father was a doctor who often demanded no payment), he had a happy childhood. In later life he married and had children, and by all accounts had a productive and satisfied life, not at all the biography of a tortured artist. He is, however, known to have had one very strange habit.

Schiller's secret to success was inspiration. He could only work when he was inspired. This seems logical, but Schiller's method for becoming inspired was perhaps less orthodox. He could only write when he was surrounded by the odor of rotting pears.

While we may not enjoy the odor of rotten fruits, there is evidence in the scientific community that humans are stimulated by scent. Each person has scents that work for them, partially because of personal taste, but also because of emotional attachments and because of memories. Modern times have let aromatherapy in the forms of candles, oils, and incense become available in nearly every fragrance you can imagine, and often at incredibly affordable prices. Lighting a scented candle or diffusing some oils might just be the thing you need to get your creative juices flowing on days when you seem stuck.

If you wish to read more on his idea, visit the Schiller Institute online:

https://schillerinstitute.com/who-is-schiller/

CHUCK INGRAHAM

Some people, like Jeannie, embrace habits from an early age and continue to be fascinated by them into adulthood. On the other hand, others tend to resist habits, for whatever reason, and employ them only in areas that are extra important, or trick themselves into habits. Habits work whether you realize you're doing them or not.

Jeannie husband, Chuck, belongs in the latter category. Despite being in the military, Chuck has resisted habits because he doesn't like anyone telling him, including his habits, what to do. However, there are certain areas that he has deemed to be extremely important and has developed habits surrounding them. For Chuck, his definition of success is having a successful family, which is healthy, both physically and emotionally. With the idea of "What small act can make the biggest difference on my family daily?", Chuck decided to bring Jeannie a cup of coffee every morning while she was still asleep.

He figures this one act helps the mother of the family wake up more peacefully, energized, and feeling loved. And it does.

Not everyone is big on habits, but if you can take something from Chuck's playbook and find one small area that has a big payoff for many areas, you can leverage the power of habits without feeling controlled by them. Maybe for you it's taking five minutes in the evening to write out a to-do list for the morning or calling your dad every night on your way home from work. Perhaps meal prepping on the weekends is the way for you.

Franz Kafka

Franz Kafka was born in Prague to a middle-class Jewish family. His background, however, was German, and as the Czech Republic was at the time part of the Austro-Hungarian Empire, he spoke and wrote exclusively in German. He's known for writing works that are bizarre, deal with unbelievable government bureaucracy, or are close to absurdist. His most famous works are *The Metamorphosis*, whose hero turns into a cockroach one morning, and *The Trial*, which centers on a man on trial for a crime that the authorities won't even name for him.

Kafka never married and was tortured by idealizations of women. He often worked as an insurance clerk, though ill health meant that most of the time he couldn't go to his office. He suffered from tuberculosis for most of his life, and the disease finally killed him at the age of forty.

The writer contributed his success to a distinctive morning ritual he had. Every morning he would spend ten minutes naked in front of his window performing a series of exercises known as the "Müller technique." And when he was finished writing, he would spend another ten minutes performing a different set of exercises. Though this might seem strange (particularly to his neighbors!), Kafka thought this ritual made his writing better. And since his books are still bestsellers, we can't argue with that!

While his particular habit may seem strange, it does underscore a general habit that has been shown to increase productivity, decrease stress, and lead to other habit formations. These groups of habits are known as start-up and shut-down routines. Whether you stand in your window naked and exercise (please warn your neighbors!), or you meditate for five minutes, clean off your desk, or enjoy a cup of tea, starting and finishing your work day with the same ritual is a beneficial habit to pursue.

More information about Kafka can be found at the Kafka Society website:

http://www.franzkafka-soc.cz/index.php?lang=en

SALVADOR DALÍ

Spanish surrealist painter Salvador Dalí is well known for his bizarre behavior. He was often seen walking around Paris with his pet anteater on a leash, for example. His work, however, speaks for itself. A talented draftsman, Dalí produced paintings that were almost lifelike but that dealt with fantastical themes. His most famous painting is *The Persistence of Memory*, with its iconic melting clocks.

Dalí's parents were convinced that Salvador was the reincarnation of his dead older brother (also called Salvador), so his upbringing was far from conventional. He did, however, lead a full and strange life, and his paintings were considered treasures even during his own lifetime. His talent was recognized early, and Dalí held his first public exhibition when he was just fourteen years old.

Arguably, Dalí's daily routine was full of weird habits that might have led to his success. But there's one habit in particular that Dalí swore by: the power nap. His version of the power nap was a very specialized one, though. He would put a metal pan on the ground, hold a steel spoon in his hand over the pan, and then doze off in his armchair. When he reached a state of total relaxation and sleep, the spoon would drop from his hand onto the pan, waking him up immediately.

Dalí used this method of napping for many years, and he said it was the reason he could be so productive. You'll also see some other successful people in this book who swear by napping. So, if the idea of waking yourself up with a clanging metal spoon doesn't sound ideal, keep reading or experiment to find your own ideal nap habit.

If you want to read more about Dalí and his pet anteater, check out this website:

https://www.salvador-dali.org/en/dali/

PYTHAGORAS

Most of us learned about the Pythagorean theorem in school, but few of us know much about the man behind the math. Pythagoras was born on the Greek island of Samos around 2500 years ago, but little is known about his early life. It's possible that his father was a gem merchant, meaning his upbringing would have been fairly wealthy, and he probably didn't leave Samos until he was already 40.

Once off the island, however, Pythagoras founded his own school and went on to make several discoveries concerning math, philosophy, and even music. Interestingly, he didn't actually invent the theorem that bears his name; instead, he and his students were the first to prove the theorem. The Pythagorean theorem had been in use as long ago as ancient Babylon.

Pythagoras put his success down to abstemious habits. In fact, he forced all students at his school to live the "Pythagorean way." This involved living a pure and simple life, and possibly being vegetarian. However, it also included some slightly stranger habits, such as never eating beans, never walking on highways, and never smoothing out the indentations a sleeping body left on bed sheets.

As strange as some of these habits may sound, purity and the lack of distraction that came along with it made Pythagoras one of the foremost minds of his day. The idea of abstinent habits has already been touched on before, and while Pythagoras's habits are a little more extreme than most of us feel comfortable with, attempting to abstain from substances or activities that distract us from our success is as important as addition habits, such as taking vitamins. Take some time and think about something that distracts you from optimal performance, and see if taking a break from it helps you in your journey. It can be anything from your morning coffee to a nightly Netflix binge.

If you want to learn more about Pythagoras and his strange followers, go to this website:

https://classicalwisdom.com/philosophy/cult-of-pythagoras/

DEMOSTHENES

Demosthenes might not be the most recognizable name nowadays, but in ancient Greece he was one of the most famous men around. An orator and lawyer, Demosthenes was born in Athens and lived a long though unhealthy life.

His interest in rhetoric and speech writing came initially out of self-need. At the age of seven, Demosthenes was orphaned, and though his father left plenty of money and a guardian for him, his guardian squandered a lot of the fortune. At the age of seventeen, Demosthenes made his first public speech, which won back what remained of his inheritance.

As anyone creative will know, getting inspired is one thing, but having the discipline to sit down and complete an idea is something else entirely. Demosthenes had a great habit that forced him to sit down and write his speeches. When he needed to focus and write, he would shave off half his hair, making himself look so ridiculous that he wouldn't be tempted to leave home.

A little drastic, perhaps, but Demosthenes was one of the most successful orators and speech writers of his day, so the head shaving definitely paid off! In line with him, many other creatives have taken drastic measures to keep them from going out, like having servants take your clothes away. On the other hand, you can do what Jeannie does and have your spouse take the car to work. No need to shave your head to keep you at home.

Find out more about the life of Demosthenes:

https://www.britannica.com/biography/Demosthenes-Greek-statesman-and-orator

VICTOR HUGO

Victor Hugo is one of the most famous French writers and one of Jeannie's all-time favorite authors and writer of her favorite book, *Les Misérables*. Additionally, Hugo wrote *The Hunchback of Notre-Dame* and other works that (thanks to a best-selling musical and a Disney film) are familiar to most of us.

Because his father was an officer in Napoleon's army, Hugo traveled a lot as a child, and his travels inspired much of his writing. His childhood was tumultuous, though, taking place during the Napoleonic Wars and the 1848 Revolutions, which were shown in his books. At the end of his life, Hugo lived in exile from Napoleon III's government.

As anyone who has read Hugo will know, his books are huge tomes numbering well over a thousand pages each. In order to complete these works, Hugo set himself daily writing goals. This in itself is a great habit to gain success, but Hugo took things further. He would write naked, giving his clothes to his valet, who could only return them once his daily writing goal was achieved.

Working in the nude might not be everyone's cup of tea, but it certainly worked for Hugo, and his books are still treasured to this day. Like Demosthenes, Hugo's habit of keeping himself at home and writing is a little extreme. Take a moment to think of what you could do in order to make it harder to not get your work done. Can you use modern approaches like programs that limit your internet use for certain periods of time, or having a friend take your TV cord so you can't binge Netflix? Low-tech solutions could be having a friend or spouse take your car keys. If you fancy having someone take your clothes like Hugo did, perhaps stick with your shoes, as most of us have too many clothes to remove and bring back daily.

More information about Victor Hugo can be found here:
https://www.victorhugoinguernsey.gg

BENJAMIN FRANKLIN

There are few American names as famous worldwide as that of Benjamin Franklin. The list of Franklin's achievements is long enough to sound almost like fantasy. From postmaster to inventor, Franklin gained success in a wide range of fields in a time before the internet made it easy and accessible.

Born to a Quaker family, he was poor but happy in his early life. There was no money to send him for proper schooling, but he educated himself through his voracious reading habit before becoming an apprentice printer. If nothing else, this habit propelled him to success; however, there are many other habits that helped Franklin, which included finding accountability and pushing himself out of his comfort zone.

While part of Franklin's success was due to his work ethic, the habit that truly led him to success was a simple one: Every morning he asked himself "What good shall I do today?" and every evening he asked himself "What good have I done today?"

This ability to reflect on one's actions is a great way to clear the mind and focus, and it assisted Benjamin Franklin in becoming the household name that he is today. Many options exist today for reflecting on your day — whether you use a simple bullet journal to keep track of your daily accomplishments, or an online system through a program like Evernote, it's never been easier to keep a journal. The key is to keep it up consistently. So pick up a pen and put it to paper.

If you want to learn more about all of Franklin's habits, because there are too many to talk about in one page, please visit the Benjamin Franklin Historical Society website:

http://www.benjamin-franklin-history.org

FRANK MCKINLEY

Writer Frank McKinley assigns his success to a very specific habit that he developed after reading *Awaken the Giant Within* by Anthony Robbins. McKinley believes the secret to his success is decision making.

The process, he explains, is a three-step one. First, he pictures what he wants in as much vivid detail as he can. Second, he decides that no matter what, he's going to go after what he wants until he gets it. Third, he accepts that the outcome of this decision making may be different from his original picture, but believes that it's best to aim high because even if you miss, you'll still get further than you would without such a lofty goal.

Though he started doing this as a young adult, only recently has he truly focused on this habit. Last fall he decided that his goal was to make it as a writer. Putting his decision-making habit to the test, he enrolled in a writer's marketing course, started his own blog, began guest blogging, and opened a Facebook writers' group. He's now on track to make writing his sole income in the next year. Could the secret to success be as simple as decision making? Frank McKinley believes so.

You can find out more about Frank McKinley at his website:
www.frankmckinleyauthor.com

JONATHAN MÜLLER

Jonathan Müller came to his habit for success after a traumatic event. While training for his beloved Brazilian jiu-jitsu, Müller ended up injured. An MRI and a doctor's appointment later and he was told never to train again. Suddenly, a major part of his life was gone; that 20 hours of training a week was no longer possible. Müller found himself plunged into depression, not working, not even doing the prescribed exercises to help his neck problem.

One morning, Müller woke up early, at 6:30 a.m., and decided to go to the gym. For the next 100 days he woke early and worked out. If there was no gym available, he went walking or did bodyweight exercises at a nearby playground. His aim was to build a habit that he could structure his life around. Initially, he intended to do this for a week. But one week became two, which became three, until he'd done a full 100 days. Though sheer perseverance he kept training, and after six months reclaimed his place in his jiu-jitsu training group.

Müller believes his success comes from structure, finding what you want to do and doing it, no excuses, no off days. Making that early-morning alarm and gym visit into a habit has meant that he's now stronger and more motivated than ever. Similar to Michal's push-up habit, Jonathan's exercise habit is a keystone habit, one that helps you develop other habits.

Maybe you don't have time to work out for an hour

every day, but one push-up or one walk around the block is doable. Pick a small exercise and do it every single day to take advantage of the same momentum that Jonathan took advantage of to get him back into training shape.

VISHNU'S VIRTUES

Vishnu, creator of the Vishnu's Virtues website, believes that his success came from a habit that's long been recommended by self-development coaches, blogs, and even some religions: meditation. Like many of us, Vishnu had always thought of meditation as boring and time-consuming. Though he was a spiritual person, meditation had never appealed to him and he found it too difficult to concentrate. However, a course with the right teacher made him realize that meditation was what his life had been lacking.

Beginning with just one minute a day, Vishnu eventually built up to eleven minutes of meditation per day over a six-month period. He found that his life was more centered, that he was calmer and more creative. If he missed a day, he didn't beat himself up; he'd just start over the next day and keep on going. He's now been meditating daily for more than three years, and it has become an essential part of his life. If he doesn't meditate, he finds that he wakes up after falling asleep, and only meditation will send him back to sleep.

Meditation is a great habit to build, and the process of starting small and achieving a little more each day has really worked for Vishnu. In addition to starting small, you can also look up different apps, like Calm or Headspace, that can help train you.

He's now a creative and successful blogger and life coach, and you can find out more about him at his website: www.vishnusvirtues.com

DAN LEIGH

Self-help author Dan Leigh thanks the productivity habit known as "Pomodoro" for his success. Leigh was frustrated by his lack of productivity as a writer, and found it so hard to get started writing each day that he often didn't write at all. Now, thanks to Pomodoro, he finds that he's more productive than ever.

Leigh first heard the Pomodoro Technique mentioned by fellow author Steve Scott. The method breaks up time into 25-minute segments, with rest breaks in between. Using a timer on his computer, Leigh now writes in 25-minute increments with five-minute breaks. Knowing that he doesn't need to commit to long, two-hour writing sessions allows Leigh to be more productive in the time that he does have. After all, 25 minutes isn't very intimidating!

The author has found that the Pomodoro method has affected many areas of his life, and he often now finds that he uses timers for tasks that he otherwise wouldn't have. But most of all, Pomodoro has helped him overcome his biggest obstacle as a writer: getting started in the morning.

*Dan Leigh is a self-help author specializing in natural health, healing, mental health, and Eastern spirituality. You can find out more about him on his website: **www.danleighpublishing.com***

DEBBIE HOROVITCH

Publicist, author, and social-media guru Debbie Horovitch can turn to only one answer when asked which habit contributed most to her success, and the answer might surprise you. Horovitch believes she has Facebooking to thank for her successful career—more specifically, Facebook networking.

Laid off from her job as an ad agency media buyer in 2007, Horovitch realized that networking and connections were what got people jobs. Using LinkedIn, she had a new job within just twelve weeks, and the networking lesson stuck with her. When she was laid off again in 2008, a mere year later, she turned to the booming social-media trend to make her connections.

Sitting at home, collecting unemployment money, socializing on Facebook, and watching Netflix, she came to the conclusion that she needed to harness the power of what she was doing to make her successful. She began adding friends on Facebook. Initially, this was fellow professionals whom she'd worked with before, but she soon moved on to adding experts in her areas of interest. Following social marketer Donnie Deutsch was a key turning point, and Horovitch found herself subscribing to his entrepreneur's training course. She then launched her own livestream show, continuing to connect with people over Facebook, including celebrity guests for her show.

Horovitch has found that her Facebook habit has developed into something that has affected every area of her life, from her career to her reputation to her self-confidence. If your job or success relies on networking, spending time on social media can beneficial. However, if you are prone to distraction, make sure you set a time limit—maybe even set a timer.

*She now specializes in book publishing and author promotion, and you can find out more about her at **debbiehorovitch.com***

FRANKIE JOHNNIE

Writer Frankie Johnnie has one mantra: Finish what you start. As a writer, she always tries to read as much as she writes, which can be difficult to find time for, but her real secret to success is always to finish what she starts.

Johnnie got tired of having so many unfinished projects, so she made a vow to always finish something once it was begun. Finding the time to do this can be tough, so she works by assigning each project a value before she begins. Higher-value projects take precedence over lower-value ones, so her time is prioritized. Nevertheless, if she starts a book, she finishes it; if she begins creating a course for writers, then she finishes it.

She has found that this habit has affected her life as a writer and as an entrepreneur. She has higher morale now, and she gets more writing done. She's found that if she can finish one project, she then has the confidence to go on and finish the next, and the next, and the next.

This trick will work great for those who always find themselves starting projects and never finishing them. On the other hand, I would suggest, for those who always finish projects, just giving yourself some time to experiment with something new. Those of us who enjoy the follow-through, as opposed to the start, can often get in ruts and feel we must finish things that will not benefit us. The key in Frankie's habit is prioritizing. Get in the habit of saying yes to only those things that will bring the most benefit to you.

*Frankie Johnnie is a teacher of all things writing, and you can find out more about her at her website: **fbkwriter.com**.*

JORDAN RING

Author Jordan Ring has a daily habit that he believes brings him true success: connecting with God. Ring prays every night before bed and does daily devotions every morning.

Although Ring has always been a Christian, he admits to never being good at reading the Bible regularly. But one day in church he was told that daily quiet time reading the word of God was a basic tenant of spiritual health. He took this message to heart and decided that he needed to make a change in his life.

Ring began slowly, just trying to ensure he picked up his Bible once a day, and found that making it the first thing he did each day was helpful. He now regularly reads the Scriptures every morning upon waking. He's found that his daily Bible reading has given him a better perspective on life and that he now approaches things in a more positive way. Ring has also found that his devotions have helped to instill in him other healthy habits, and that he is constantly reminded that his need for God trumps any earthly desire.

Habit building has been key for Ring, and he attributes his success in life to his daily habit of reading the Bible. While not all our readers will be Christian, delving into sacred texts daily is a tenet of most religions. Many religions also emphasize meditation practices, like prayer, as a daily habit as well. Science has shown that habits such as these have the power to transform your brain. Even those with no formal religious affiliation can benefit from these two habits of reading sacred texts and meditation. These texts have enduring wisdom that is applicable to even modern man, and meditation has taken hold in even the most secular, atheistic cultures.

You can find out more about Jordan Ring and his work at **jmring.com***.*

PATRIK EDBLAD

Swedish writer and trainer Patrik Edblad has had his articles published by some of the biggest names on the Web, but being successful hasn't always been easy. For a long time, Edblad found that his natural tendency toward being disorganized meant that he was dealing reactively with problems rather than proactively.

All that changed, however, when Edblad developed a habit of holding a weekly planning session. Every Sunday, Edblad sets aside thirty minutes to an hour to go over the previous week and plan the following week. During this time he handles the mundane (making sure all his electronics are charged so that Monday morning he'll be ready to go), but also important things such as self-praise (writing down three to five accomplishments from the previous week), which he finds helps to motivate him. He also analyzes where things have gone wrong in the previous week and goes over his schedule for the next week, as well as tidying up his workspace.

Edblad says that this planning session is one of the most powerful habits that he's developed in recent years, and it surely contributes to his success. But it's important to be flexible and to allow your weekly planning to change over time to fit your current needs. This may mean you decide to take some time on Sunday night like Edblad, or choose to review your week at the end on a Friday.

You can find out more about Patrik Edblad and his work at **patrikedblad.com.**

ALEXANDRA KOROTKOVA

Russian-to-English translator Alexandra Korotkova wasn't always as successful in her field as she is today; in fact, there was a time when she spoke no English at all. A study-abroad trip to the States sparked a love of the English language, but upon arriving home, Korotkova found that she still didn't understand English as well as she wanted to.

So she began a new habit: listening to audiobooks in English. At first this was very difficult—the lack of visuals such as facial expressions and gestures made understanding tough, and after five minutes or so of listening, Korotkova was exhausted. After a month or two, however, Korotkova found that she could listen to books, podcasts, and audio even while commuting and for as long as she liked.

Korotkova is now an English-to-Russian translator focusing on book and film translation. If it hadn't been for her habit, she'd never have been able to do the job that she now loves. And she still listens to audiobooks, just for pleasure.

STEPHEN KING

Stephen King is one of the best-known names in the writing world. A prolific author, King has written dozens of books from hard-core horror to fantasy and fairy tales. But things weren't always like this. King once wallpapered a wall in his office with rejection letters from publishers and magazines.

King attributes his success to the habit of having habits. That might sound strange, but King thinks that a writer should build habits around his writing in the same way as you would for any other routine activity. To this end he starts work at the same time every day, he makes sure his papers are in the same order and the same place, he takes his vitamin pill and drinks some tea, and he gets to work. Clearly King is in the camp of those who fully embrace habits.

The purpose of all of this, King says, is to make writing a part of your routine. When he goes through his ritual of sitting in the same seat and taking his vitamin pill, his brain knows that it's time to get to work.

Building habits and routines is important even if you're creative, and Stephen King's amazing success as an author just goes to prove that. Whether we realize it or not, our brain revolves around habits. Once you learn how to drive and drive for a while, you can get in your car and hardly have a conscious thought until you get to your destination. With picking habits and engraining them, we get to prioritize what we want consciously, instead of our unconscious brain just picking the easiest route. In that case, you might end up with a bad habit of hitting the snooze button ten times and arriving at work unsettled and possibly a few minutes late.

If you're interested in learning more about his writing, or his *thoughts on writing, visit his website: **www.stephenking.com***

STEVE JOBS

When Steve Jobs, founder of Apple, died, he was worth eleven billion dollars. That's not bad for a guy who started a company in a garage. Jobs was undoubtedly one of the foremost visionaries in tech, and his success is undeniable.

What habits led to Jobs's success? He was vegan, and lived a relatively simple life. He'd eat only one kind of food, for example, for weeks before switching to a different food and doing the same again, meaning he didn't even have to waste time deciding what to have for lunch. But the one key trait that many people believed made Jobs the success that he was, was his ethos to always be true to himself.

Every morning Jobs would spend a few minutes looking at himself in a mirror and ask: "If today was the last day of my life, would I be happy with what I'm about to do today?" If the answer to the question was no, then he knew that he needed to change something.

Jobs's morning habit kept him feeling good about himself, and this meant that he could work with a clear conscience knowing that what he was doing was making him happy. This is an important lesson. Being successful is all very well, but being happy is more important. And in this case, being satisfied with what he did certainly contributed to Steve Jobs's success.

To see his lasting impressions, visit the Apple page they set up in memoriam: ***https://www.apple.com/stevejobs/***

BARACK OBAMA

There's no denying that Barack Obama is a successful man. Charismatic and intelligent, the first African American president of the United States is a strong believer in family, and his daily routines reflect this.

Rising early, working out, reading the papers, and then breakfasting with his family, Obama made time to take his children to school even when serving as a senator. Though he often works late into the night, he will still make time for family dinners. A good work-life balance is key to success, but Obama also has another secret habit that has contributed to achieving his ambitions.

The ex-president has the habit of simplifying everything—to the point that he has a "personal uniform" that he wears each day to avoid wasting time making decisions about what he will wear. His morning routine of working out, reading, and breakfasting before getting down to business is as simple as it gets.

Sometimes building a habit is about subtracting the unimportant, rather than adding something new. There's nothing fancy in Obama's schedule, but maybe that's the real key to his success. Taking away the unimportant things leaves more time to focus on the things that need to be prioritized. Maybe your morning routine could use a simplification makeover. Make sure that you make time in the morning for what is most important to you.

To find out what the former president is up to, visit his website:

https://barackobama.com/

BILL GATES

Businessman, investor, and philanthropist Bill Gates is one of the richest men in the world, despite being a college dropout. His programming experience and innovations have affected most of us, and you probably won't be able to go through your day without using at least some of Gates's code.

Bill Gates's secret to success is a very simple one: he never stops learning. Even as a child, he was an inveterate bookworm. In fact, he read so much that his parents had to ban books at the dinner table. Every year, Gates releases a list of his must-read books that cover everything from science to fiction.

Nowadays, Gates takes his learning to a new level every morning. The tycoon's morning routine is simple. He gets up after at least seven hours of sleep (he believes getting enough sleep is important for his energy levels) and spends an hour on the treadmill. This workout time isn't wasted, though. While exercising, he watches online courses from The Teaching Company on everything from geology to U.S. history.

Gates knows that even the most successful people never stop learning, something that has helped keep him ahead of the game and on top of growing trends. You can start your own learning process by watching TED Talks, listening to podcasts, and reading important books. Or you can even watch the Netflix documentary on his brain, called *Inside Bill's Brain:*

https://www.youtube.com/watch?v=aCv29JKmHNY

OPRAH WINFREY

Media mogul, TV star, actress, magazine editor, and author Oprah Winfrey is one of the biggest and most influential names in America. But she wasn't always successful. Born to an unwed teenaged mother, Oprah spent the early years of her life living in rural poverty. Sexually abused by family members, at the age of just 14 she gave birth to a son who died shortly thereafter. However, despite all this, Oprah has grown to become not only a familiar household name, but also one of the richest women in America.

The habit that Oprah attributes to her success is meditation, which she says allows her to separate herself from the "daily craziness" of the world around her. Twice a day, every day, for twenty minutes, Oprah sits and meditates. She practices transcendental meditation as preached by Maharishi Mahesh Yogi, which uses the sound of a chanted mantra to calm and relax.

Taking a little time out from a busy schedule is important, and means that when you return to work, you are in a more relaxed and happier mental state. Oprah says that her meditation time leaves her feeling full of hope and joy.

Visit Oprah's website, ***http://www.oprah.com/index.html,*** *to find out more about her habits and practices.*

REED HASTINGS

The founder and CEO of Netflix is many things one would expect, such as incredibly wealthy, but one area in which he seems to buck trends within American corporate culture is that of vacations. It seems wherever you look, Americans are putting more and more time in at work, but Hastings thinks this thinking is backward.

Currently, at Netflix, the office has an unlimited parental leave and vacation policy. If you want, or need, time off, you can take it without being penalized. Recently he told Entrepreneur.com, "Most of us are so wrapped around efficiency in management that we don't sufficiently value flexibility. We're willing to take some inefficiency narrowly and in edge cases to create an environment that's extremely flexible because we think that outperforms in the long term."

Hastings sets the example himself. He takes an average of two weeks off per quarter, or six weeks per year, which is about three to four times the average American's time off. Currently, Netflix accounts for 39% of all internet traffic between nine p.m. and midnight and is worth almost $40 billion, more than any of the major networks like CBS, which doesn't have as generous of a leave policy.

It may not be possible for you to take six weeks off per year, but it's still important to find down time. Most employers offer leave, but often employees don't take full advantage of it. Even if a vacation in some location, either exotic or closer to home, isn't within your means, take a staycation to putter around your house or play tourist in your home city. And if you have no available leave, take advantage of your time off from work by fully disconnecting.

To learn more about Reed and how he grew his company, check out his profile on Forbes:

https://www.forbes.com/profile/reed-hastings/#edb42f827829

ERNEST HEMINGWAY

Ernest Hemingway is one of the world's most famous writers. American born, Hemingway traveled extensively, spending much of his time in Europe during World War I, and hunting in Africa. His brief, economic style of writing is iconic, and his novels from *The Sun Also Rises* to *For Whom the Bell Tolls* are classics, read by high school students the world over. Jeannie gathered much of her early writing style from Hemingway, enjoying his sparse-but-engaging prose.

Like many writers, Hemingway had distinctive habits for how his writing routine worked. Unlike many writers, however, Hemingway only wrote for short periods every day. He would wake up early, at sunrise, and begin work. He wrote only during the morning, often stopping way before lunch. For the rest of the day he would forbid himself from writing, allowing ideas to percolate and inspiration to come. This resulted in him being excited to write the next morning. This would work well if you are the type of person who needs time to let ideas sink in, especially if you keep a little ideas notebook, or Evernote, in your pocket to keep track of flashes of brilliance.

Hemingway ensured that his prose remained fresh and that he had plenty of time to get inspiration. Not everyone, however, is an early bird, and you can pick a time at night or in the afternoon to write. Hemingway's basic idea was to limit the time, and only engage in writing at that time, to keep him excited about writing and give his brain time to process.

*Learn about Hemingway and about some more of his often off-the-wall habits here: **https://www.hemingwaysociety.org/***

JENNIFER ANISTON

Jennifer Aniston is one of the most recognizable faces in entertainment. A cast member of the hit '90s show *Friends* as well as a star of plenty of hit movies, Aniston is loved all around the world. The child of two actors, Aniston always knew that her career lay on the screen.

Her habit for success is a tough one to follow. She wakes at 4:30 in the morning, drinks hot water with lemon, washes her face, and then spends twenty minutes meditating. Breakfast is a simple protein shake, after which she spends thirty minutes on her exercise bike and a further forty minutes doing yoga. And after all that? She hits the gym.

Aniston's habits definitely contribute to keeping her slim figure and youthful appearance. But getting the hard work of exercising done early in the morning leaves the rest of the day free for work and other activities. And the buzz of endorphins from all that exercise leaves her fresh and full of energy. Sure, it's all hard work, but it obviously pays off, as Jennifer Aniston is hugely successful in her career.

As stated elsewhere in this book, getting your priorities in early in the day helps set a positive tone for the rest of the day. Exercise is one of those cornerstone habits that helps you develop other good habits, and it also helps give you a burst of energy that even coffee can't compare with. Daily meditation and exercise help keep her body and mind sharp. Think about what you could do first thing in the morning that will contribute to your body and mind. Even if you don't have a couple of hours, fitting in a push-up like Michal and five minutes of prayer and meditation will set you on the path to success.

If you want to read more about Aniston and her lifestyle, visit her website: ***http://jennifer-aniston.org/***

MAYA ANGELOU

Poet, autobiographer, and civil-rights activist Maya Angelou is a name familiar to most Americans. She recited her poetry at the inauguration of Bill Clinton, was a professor, and won more than 50 awards and honors over her lifetime, including the Presidential Medal of Freedom. The author of *I Know Why the Caged Bird Sings* survived being abandoned by her parents to her grandmother's care, being sexually abused by her stepfather, and was mute for five years after her stepfather was murdered. But she went on to become one of the most influential African Americans of the twentieth century.

Angelou's habit for success involved minimizing distraction. In order to write, she would rent a hotel room, far away from the calls of her everyday life. The room was as minimalistic as possible, containing only a Bible, a pack of cards, and a bottle of sherry. In this room she would write every day from seven in the morning until two in the afternoon.

Making a separate space for work away from any distractions allowed Angelou to focus solely on her writing. And the result was some of the most powerful literature in America. While renting a hotel room or separate space may not always be possible, as it certainly wasn't in her early career, you can still find a specific, distraction-free place to do your work, whether it's writing, running a business, or painting. Jeannie has been known to lock herself in the bathroom with her laptop when she has a big writing deadline, which is actually a popular move of many mothers. Jeannie learned the trick from a writing professor and from her grandmother, also named Jeannie, who was completely available for her family at all hours except for an hour and a half that she had her bath time every night.

To learn more about Maya Angelou's legacy, visit **https://www.mayaangelou.com**

EMINEM

Hit rap artist and actor Eminem—or Marshall Mathers, to use his real name—is one of the most powerful musicians in modern America. Renowned for his rhyming skills and speed, Eminem is the proud owner of an Oscar and fifteen Grammy awards.

After his parents' divorce, Eminem grew up the child of a single mother. Letters he sent to his father were returned unopened. The two moved frequently, rarely staying in one place for long, and Eminem was bullied as a child, once so badly that he had severe head injuries. He repeated ninth grade three times before dropping out of school. He's had plenty of legal trouble, suffered drug dependency, and has bipolar disorder. But with the launch of his first album followed by the release of the film *8 Mile*, Eminem became one of the most popular rap artists of all time.

Eminem's habit for success is a simple one: sleep. The rapper believes that a full, uninterrupted night of sleep is key to keeping his energy levels and creativity high. When staying in a hotel, Eminem orders the windows to be covered in aluminum foil for complete darkness, and speakers to be installed so he can play ambient music throughout the night. According to him, this ensures the best night of sleep.

Getting a good night's sleep is an excellent habit to have, and one that rapper Eminem thinks is responsible for his astounding success. No late-night partying and clubbing for Eminem; he'll be under the comforter snoring instead! His habit of sleep is even more important for those with mental illnesses. Perhaps one of Eminem's greatest strengths is in knowing his limitations. For those with physical or mental illnesses, getting proper sleep on a schedule is a cornerstone to maintaining your health.

Want to learn more about Eminem? Check out his website:
https://www.eminem.com/

SERENA WILLIAMS

Serena Williams is one of America's foremost sportswomen. An unbelievable tennis player, she's been ranked number 1 in the world no less than eight times. She's won 39 Grand Slam titles and held all four singles Grand Slam titles simultaneously!

The youngest of five sisters, Serena began playing tennis when she was three years old. Home schooled for most of her childhood, she has devoted her life to tennis. However, her upbringing was a happy one. Though her parents home schooled and coached her, she remembers that they allowed her time to be a child, and even stopped sending her to tournaments when she was ten so she could have a more normal childhood.

Serena's habit for success is a fairly simple one: dedication and hard work. Even during childhood, she would practice at six o'clock, do her school lessons, and then play again. There is no substitute for hard work and discipline, and Serena Williams is proof that ingraining those habits is the key to success.

It can be hard to think of hard work as a habit, but if your body and mind are accustomed to putting in effort, it actually seems like less effort in the long run. Perhaps trying to go from couch potato to practicing your endeavor several hours per day may be too much, but slowly increasing your time spent can help you go from zero to hero with less effort than you imagine.

Serena has even channeled her hard work into other endeavors, such as her growing fashion line, which can be found online at **serenawilliams.com/**

ARIANNA HUFFINGTON

Columnist, entrepreneur, and author Arianna Huffington is a media mogul. She's on the Forbes list of most influential women in media, she was the founder of website The Huffington Post, and is now the head of start-up Thrive Global. The Greek-American billionaire is a controversial figure, but there's no denying that she's successful.

Huffington puts her success down to four habits, all relatively simple ones. She ensures that she gets enough sleep, she eats healthily, she exercises, and she meditates. These she calls the foundation of her success. Only when she balances her busy work life with sleep, good food, meditation, and exercise can she be at her most productive.

The simplicity of Huffington's habits is deceptive. She's actually laying the ground work for her success by looking after herself, something that many of us forget to do, especially when we're pushing ourselves to succeed. Get to bed on time, eat right, and spend some time looking after your mind and your body, and you'll put yourself in the position to attain success.

These four habits are all keystone habits, which we've already touched on briefly. Why these habits make such a difference, science can't tell us for sure. But these specific habits all increase your energy levels and clarity of mind. Maybe you don't need nine hours of sleep or a vegan diet doesn't sit well with you, but making sure you take care of your body should always be your top priority.

Arianna, nicknamed the sleep evangelist, is very open about the need for sleep, which she has written a book about, and is splashed all over the first page of her website:

http://ariannahuffington.com

MARK PARKER

Mark Parker is the head of Nike, and he joined the company as a mere designer before ascending to CEO. He's estimated to earn around $15 million per year (making him the fourteenth-highest-paid CEO in America), and in 2015 was *Fortune's* businessman of the year.

The habit that Parker says contributes most to his success involves note taking. He carries a notebook everywhere he goes, allowing him to remember everything he's told, or any idea he has. But he fills his notebook in a very particular way. The left-hand pages are devoted to writing, while the right-hand pages are for sketches only. This, Parker says, allows him to balance his brain. Perhaps it's no surprise that someone who started out as a designer also needs to present information in sketch format, and it certainly works for Parker.

Note taking is a fantastic habit, since it allows you to keep track of everything you need without having to remember things, and it lets your brain cells concentrate on other areas, like idea development. Parker's habit of both sketching and writing information is also a great way to ensure that information is not only understood, but also digested better.

Learn how Mark Parker is disrupting corporate culture in this article:
https://www.bizjournals.com/portland/news/2018/09/20/nike-ceo-mark-parker-addresses-toxic-culture.html

J.K. ROWLING

J.K. Rowling is one of the biggest names in modern literature. Her best-selling Harry Potter franchise has been turned into blockbuster films and translated into dozens of languages. She's a billionaire, and at one point was the richest woman in the world (though she's now donated a significant portion of her wealth to charity).

Famously, Rowling wrote most of her best-selling books as a poor single mother, often working in cafés. She also lost her mother during the writing process. The first book in the series, *Harry Potter and the Philosopher's Stone,* was rejected by twelve major publishers before finally finding a home with Bloomsbury Press.

Rowling says the habit that led her to success is that of preparation and planning. The idea for Harry Potter came to her on a train journey, but she didn't begin writing the first book for a very long time. Instead, she spent a full five years planning out the story and each individual book before putting pen to paper.

Planning and preparation are habits that allow you to develop ideas in a more controlled environment, and J.K. Rowling's stunning success just goes to show that time spent planning is very valuable indeed. The old axiom states, "If you don't know where you are going, you'll always miss the mark." Whether you're writing a book or starting a business, having a plan, even if it's more basic than Rowling's, will ensure you hit your mark.

Learn more about the writing icon's life at
https://www.jkrowling.com/about/

THOMAS EDISON

Businessman and inventor Thomas Edison is familiar to most of us. The inventor of hundreds of things, from the movie camera to the lightbulb, and holder of thousands of patents, Edison is often referred to as the greatest American inventor of all time.

The youngest of seven children, Edison was born in Ohio and raised in Michigan after a brief time in Canada. He attended school for only a few months, thereafter being taught by his mother at home, and simultaneously working to help support his large family. Edison got his start selling newspapers and candy to train passengers. He went on to found Menlo Park, a great center of innovation and invention in New Jersey, and died both wealthy and successful.

The habit that Edison credited for his success stemmed from his belief that to have one great idea, you had to come up with hundreds of ideas. Quantity wins out over quality every time. To this end he set idea quotas for all of his staff. For himself he set the goal of one minor invention every ten days, and a major invention every six months.

Goal setting is a great habit to have, helping maintain motivation and keep steady progress. It took Edison over 9,000 experiments and ideas before he perfected the lightbulb. But because he set himself steady goals, he didn't give up. And making sure he entertained different ideas, even if they didn't really pan out in the end, was also integral to his success. Part of this is knowing when to cut the cord when an idea isn't working. Maybe you start a business with ten products, but two of them don't sell well. Not every invention can be a lightbulb. But if you don't keep trying new things, you'll never find your lightbulb.

If you want to learn more about the lasting impact of Edison and his inventions, check out this PBS special on him:

https://www.pbs.org/wgbh/theymadeamerica/whomade/ edison_hi.html

Novak Djokovic

Novak Djokovic is a Serbian tennis player, currently ranked fourteenth in the world, and winner of an impressive twelve Grand Slam titles. He's won six Australian Open titles, three from Wimbledon, two from the U.S. Open, and a French Open title as well.

Born in Belgrade to a Croatian father and Montenegrin mother, Djokovic is one of three sons, all of whom are professional tennis players. He began playing tennis when he was only four years old, and began his international tennis career when he was just fourteen.

Djokovic puts his success on the tennis circuit down to three habits he developed early in his career. The first is to always drink a large glass of water immediately after waking up to hydrate after eight hours of sleep. The second is to eat two tablespoons of honey per day. And the third is to keep a strict, gluten-free diet.

Keeping hydrated and eating healthily aren't just important for sportsmen. Whatever your profession, staying healthy means more energy and better results. While a gluten-free diet may not be for everyone (says Jeannie the celiac with a severe, life-threatening response to gluten), strict diets can be helpful to many people. Some people find habits easier to maintain if they are all or nothing. If you find yourself being unable to eat just one cookie from the box, maybe this approach is for you. Whether you set up the rule of "I never eat processed sugar" or "I never eat red meat," these all-or-nothing dietary rules have clear-cut guidelines and built-in fail-safes. On the other hand, if you *can* only eat one cookie, this approach may be too strict for you. And you can try one of Djokovic's other habits, like drinking water first thing in the morning.

Novak Djokovic can be found at:
http://novakdjokovic.com/en/

RAY ALLEN

Basketball player Ray Allen is now retired, but he was a powerhouse on the basketball court. Playing most notably for the Boston Celtics and Miami Heat, Allen is considered one of the most accurate free-throw and three-point shooters of all time. He's achieved the status of NBA All Star ten times, and won two NBA championships.

The middle child out of five, Allen was a military kid and grew up all over the world. When he eventually settled in California to go to high school, he was bullied due to the strange accent he'd picked up while living in Britain. His athletic skills soon made him popular, however, and he was picked up by the University of Connecticut once he graduated from high school. The fifth pick of the 1996 draft, Allen began playing for the Milwaukee Bucks and went on to have a highly successful and profitable pro career.

Allen says his basketball success is due to a strict habit of routine he built up to pre-game. Before every game he would nap for ninety minutes, eat a light meal of chicken and rice, and then go out to play.

Building up energy by taking power naps is an excellent way to improve focus and productivity, not just to build athletic prowess. Making a nap part of your day can mean accomplishing more, especially if you don't always get enough sleep at night.

To learn more about Ray, visit his website:
https://www.ray34.com/

MICHAEL HYATT

Michael Hyatt is a success by anyone's definition of the word. The ex-chairman of Thomas Nelson Publishers, Hyatt is now an entrepreneur and author, with his company appearing on the Inc. 5000 list of the fastest-growing companies in America.

Hyatt attributes his success to having a strong morning routine that sets him up for the most productive day possible. This routine is made up of a series of habits. First, he never schedules anything before eight in the morning, giving him time to set his day up properly. Second, the night before, he prepares himself for his day. This includes using an app to set out his three main priorities for the next day, opening up the programs he'll need on his computer, setting out his exercise clothes, and getting to bed on time.

Michael Hyatt knows that success comes from preparation. His habits help make his mornings run smoothly so that he can get down to work. And when he does work, he's more productive than ever.

If you are an author, or someone looking to increase their online platform, check out his program ***www.platformuniversity.com***

BRAD LOMENICK

Speaker, leadership consultant, author, and founder of BLINC Brad Lomenick specializes in leadership, personal growth, and innovation. The entrepreneur also runs a movement known as Catalyst to teach and inspire youth to become leaders.

While Lomenick has more than twenty habits that he believes make a great leader, there are three major ideas that he says inspire success. The first is the habit of curiosity: a great leader always strives for knowledge. The second is self-discovery, in order that you know yourself better and how you work to better become successful. The third is the habit of innovation, seeking new ideas and new ways of doing things.

Will Lomenick's habits enable you to become president? Perhaps. But even if they don't, these leadership habits will certainly lead to more success in your day-to-day life. Brad's habits underlie the major themes behind most keystone habits.

To learn more about Brad's style of leadership and how to grow as a leader, visit his website:

http://www.bradlomenick.com/

JEFF GOINS

Best-selling author Jeff Goins has written many books on how to be successfully creative, including *The Art of Work* and *Real Artists Don't Starve*. When not writing about creativity, he manages Tribe Writers, an online community of authors.

Like many other successful people, Goins ascribes to the habit of lifelong learning. While this habit is important for all people, lifelong is especially important for creative types. In order to find inspiration, it is necessary to continually keep your eyes peeled. Creativity and inspiration never appear out of thin air. As Jeannie says to people who want to be writers, you have to be a reader first. The more widely you read, the better a writer you will become. Some of the most creative thinkers of our times—whether in science, technology, or politics—are known for reading far out of their comfort zones.

Constant learning can be accomplished in many ways—by reading, even with online courses. But developing the habit of being a lifelong learner will definitely produce results. You can even read some of Jeff's work or join one of his communities.

If you'd like to learn about the groups or programs that Jeff offers, visit his website: ***https://goinswriter.com/hello/***

CASS SUNSTEIN

Lawyer Cass Sunstein has developed programs for Harvard University, testified before Senate hearings, written books, and worked at the White House. He is the author of *Nudge*, a book about decision making and habit formation.

Sunstein believes that good habit formation comes from setting simple, easy-to-follow rules. For example, if you want to make keeping fit a habit, then it helps to run, or play squash with the same partner, at the same time every day. His personal habit that he finds leads to greater productivity and therefore better success is to set aside a time each day for writing. Between nine and twelve every morning, Sunstein can be found at his desk.

Making habits routine, rather than trying to fit things in where you can, is a great way of sticking to them. Cass Sunstein knows this, which is why he's an expert in his field.

To find out more about Cass and how to automate your habits with simple rules, visit the Nudge website:

http://nudges.org

CHARLES DUHIGG

Charles Duhigg is considered by many to be one of foremost authorities on habits and their formations. Duhigg doesn't often talk about his own habits, but he uses his keen observation skills as a journalist to see others' habits and the effects they have. The habits that lead to success don't necessarily have to be your own habits. Observing those of others can bring you an equal amount of success. Duhigg recalls a story from his time as a journalist in Iraq during a time when civilian rebellions and riots were common.

An army major in a particular Iraqi city observed the habits that led up to these riots, noticing that riots developed in the same way every time. First people would show up in an open space like a plaza, then more would come, then more, and eventually someone would throw a bottle or a rock and the riot would begin. So the major ordered that all food vendors be banned from the town's main square.

Several days later, crowds began to gather in the square in a way that would usually foretell a riot. More and more people came, the sun began to set, and the crowd became hungry. Unfortunately, the normal food sellers weren't there. So, gradually, people began to leave. There was no riot that night.

The army major, schooled in the power of habit by the military, was quick to notice the habits of others. And in this particular case, his observations meant that he was able to avoid potential civilian violence. Knowing the habits of others can be instrumental in climbing the ladder to success.

If you are interested in reading Duhigg's seminal work on habits, *The Power of Habits,* we can guarantee you won't regret it. His ideas are well researched and supported by science, and he is in fact the first one to popularize the concept of keystone habits.

You can find his book on Amazon and in all major and minor bookstores:

https://www.amazon.com/dp/B006WAIV6M/

ALCOA

Sometimes success requires changing the habits of others rather than your own, and Alcoa is a great example of this. In the 1980s the aluminum-manufacturing giant was on the rocks. They'd had several failed product lines, and profits were falling. Then along came Paul O'Neill.

O'Neill was appointed CEO of Alcoa in 1987, and in October of that year he gave his first speech to his investors. Rather than talking about profit margins or revenue, O'Neill instead talked about worker safety. He announced that he planned to have zero worker injuries in coming years.

Investors panicked, thinking that O'Neill was crazy and deluded. However, a year later, while employee injuries had decreased, profits had increased. Immensely. What had started as simply examining work safety strategies had spiraled into improving productivity and efficiency as well. What O'Neill had realized was that in order to change the company, he had to start small. By encouraging his workers to focus on habits that made them and others safer, he had also forced his employees to look at all their other work habits, with impressive results.

When O'Neill retired, thirteen years later, profits at Alcoa were five times higher than they had been in 1987. O'Neill knew that habits make success and that changing habits starts one step at a time.

Check out where Alcoa is now by visiting their website:
https://www.alcoa.com/global/en/home.asp

OLIVER TRUONG

Student and writer Oliver Truong has what might seem like a very strange habit that he says has led to his success. Every morning, Truong takes an ice-cold shower.

What on earth would provoke someone to do something like that? Well, Truong had the same initial distaste for the idea. He initially thought he could never take icy showers, but the idea was to purposefully challenge himself, to put himself in an uncomfortable situation. So he took a cold shower. And the next morning he did it again. And after a week he wondered if he could do it for another week, so he did, and so on.

Truong found that he used to believe that his goals were unachievable. But by purposefully doing something he thought he couldn't do, he proved himself able. The mind-set that caused him to take his ice-cold showers has now bled into the rest of his life. So taking that first cold shower was only the first step in changing his outlook on life. Now, Truong says, he can accomplish anything he puts his mind to!

To find more wisdom from Oliver visit him on Quora:
https://www.quora.com/profile/Oliver-Truong-1

GUARI SAJU

Gauri Saju didn't have a miserable life, but it wasn't entirely happy either. She says most of the time her emotions were unstable and got the best of her on many occasions. With a busy life and job, she didn't feel like she had an awful lot of time to commit to exercise. She also didn't find the appeal of going to the gym. So like many introverts who want to exercise, she decided to walk.

Her habit started with the purchase of a new pair of headphones. She would simply walk to and from work, which she estimates is about two miles, while she listens to a play list of her favorite music. To her surprise, the daily walks have dramatically improved her emotional stability. Gauri combined a cue reward, listening to her music, with a habit, which has allowed it to stick easier. Additionally, music has also shown to increase mood.

Gauri suggests that everyone find a way to exercise daily, whether it's at a gym, in a sports group, or a solo activity like walking, not just for physical but also for mental and emotional help. It's why people often go for walks to clear their heads.

To get more wisdom from Guari, visit her on Quora:
https://www.quora.com/profile/Gauri-Saju

MATT SANDRINI

Matt Sandrini used to feel like he had no time to do any of the activities he wanted to do, such as journal or read. No matter what he did, no positive habit would stick. He eventually realized all of this was due to one single bad habit: overuse of his smartphone.

Now, every night at 9:15, he has an alarm go off on his smartphone, which says it's "Amish time." And then he turns off his technology. He says, "This 5-second tiny habit made the biggest difference."

Since instating daily Amish time, Sandrini has started to get through his reading list, journal, and meditate. And without the disrupting light and buzz from his phone, he's had the added benefit of deeper sleep.

It's very easy to let technology take over your life, especially in the name of efficiency or self-improvement. While technology can be a great asset, sometimes we spend more time getting the last drop of efficiency out of ourselves, and it, that we actually use more time or get sucked into attention economy, where companies do whatever they can to keep your brain hooked into their app for as long as possible. Follow the 80/20 rule, which is that 80% of your results come from 20% of your activities, and take a look at which apps, programs, and tech bring you 80% of your results. You'll probably find that 80% comes from only 20% of your technology-involved activities.

The alternate is also true: 80% of your wasted time probably comes from 20% of your activities. If you want to find the time like Matt, cut out the biggest time wasters, which for Matt was his late-night smartphone habit.

To learn more on how to increase your available time, visit Matt's site:

https://www.timezillionaire.com

BRIAN BUFFINI

Brian, an Irishman, arrived in the United States as a 19-year old with $93 in his pocket. Just two weeks later, he was run by a car and spent two years in hospitals, ending up with over $200,000 debt in medical bills. First, he started doing what he knew from Ireland, which was working in his family business: commercial and residential painting. With the debt gnawing at him, Brian took an interest in real estate. And it really paid off! At the age of 26, he was a millionaire.

Nowadays, Brian Buffini owns the biggest coaching company in the USA (and 40+ other businesses). Since speaking and teaching is his core business, he gets a question about his secret to success very often. Brian attributes most of his results to the habit of writing personal notes. Because he keeps his notes short and to the point, every day, he writes 10 of them.

Like many other habits, Brian secludes himself from outside influences. Right before writing the note, Brian closes his eyes and visualizes the person he is writing to and asks himself a series of questions:

- Do they have a need?
- What are they going through? What they are experiencing in their life?
- What they are into?
- How can I make this person's day?

He testifies that this habit allowed him to crave some fantastic connections, for example, he was able to convince Neil Amstrong to speak at one of his event. Brian states that no other habit in his business has taken him less time, cost less money and produced bigger results than writing personal notes.

You should try it yourself. It doesn't just bring more business. It amplifies your relationships with others and makes you instantly feel better. It's a perfect habit to include in your morning ritual. And you never know, you could end up writing a book with a Polish accountant, getting an email from Tina Fey, or shaking hands with the great Neil Armstrong!

You can connect with Brian Buffini through his fantastic podcast: The Brian Buffini Show:

https://www.thebrianbuffinishow.com/

NG JUN SIANG

Teacher Ng Jun Siang has found that conscious habits are a great way to achieve success. This is an idea that may be unfamiliar to some people, but Siang picked up the idea in the military.

In everyday life we're faced with millions of choices all the time, and making the correct choice often takes willpower. However, in the military, Siang found that certain drills always took place the same way; there were no choices. Siang began to use these drills in his everyday life. So, for example, when his alarm clock goes off, he gets up. No snoozing; no lying in bed. There's no choice involved; it's just an unquestioned habit.

Siang has found that by instituting these conscious habits, he not only saves time but also saves energy and willpower for the choices that do need to be made. By using this idea of "you don't have a choice," Siang makes his life more streamlined and simpler. And that's definitely a habit that can make you successful!

Take a moment and think about what choices you could remove from your life. It doesn't have to be getting up with the first alarm, but it's a good habit, which many military members seem to be unable to shake even decades after the military. Just ask Jeannie's habit-defying husband! Maybe you always have an egg for breakfast. Or you immediately put your running shoes on when you get out of bed.

To get more wisdom from Ng Jun Siang, visit him on Quora:
https://www.quora.com/profile/Ng-Jun-Siang

NELSON WANG

Nelson Wang came across his habit quite by accident. According to his answer to a Quora question on small habits that changed lives, Nelson learned to reframe what he thought as annoyances and then even what could be seen as traumas.

First, the radiator in his apartment made a loud, banging sound at six a.m. After repeated attempts to get it fixed with no answer from the building super, he decided to reframe it from an annoyance to an insistent alarm clock. He decided that he would just always wake up at six a.m. Later, when a friend died and he dipped into depression, he decided to reframe the loss as a call to action. Now he reminds himself that he needs to take advantage of every moment as his friend had encouraged him to do.

Reframing is an easy habit to develop. And it's an easy way to help you develop other habits. Reframing gave Nelson the new habit of getting up early every day and exercising, which is another keystone habit.

Is there something in your life that you could reframe? Maybe a child jumping on your bed at six a.m. is an annoyance that you can funnel into making a healthy breakfast for both of you?

To find out more about Nelson's habits and his successes, follow him on his blog: https://www.ceolifestyle.io/

RADU TOMULEASA

Radu Tomuleasa has a very simple habit that he says leads to success. It's called the two-minute rule. If something takes less than two minutes, you have to do it immediately.

For example, if you receive an email and a response to that email will take you less than two minutes, you should write the response now, not later. Or if there's a dirty plate on the table, washing it or putting it in the dishwasher takes less than two minutes, so it needs to be done immediately. The idea of the two-minute rule is that it stops tasks from piling up.

Tomuleasa has found that instituting the two-minute rule has had all kinds of positive effects on his life, from a cleaner living space to a less cluttered mind. Such a simple habit, and one that takes very little time, is a great precursor to success.

The two-minute rule is almost a ubiquitous piece of advice in the modern world. Wherever you seem to turn, someone gives you that piece of advice. Why wait to do it if it takes you less than two minutes to do? Where did the rule start? Later in this book we'll introduce you to the man who brought it into American, and even worldwide, consciousness with the book *Getting Things Done*.

The two-minute rule works 90% of the time. The only time it seems to break down is when you have a job or lifestyle where most things take less than two minutes to do, and you have a lot of them, but also suffer from constant, or near constant, interruptions. A prime example seems to be a stay-at-home parents of young children. So unless you have a toddler and baby who dumped Cheerios all over the floor, dumped dishwashing soap into your carpet, and are currently trying to chew through your electrical cords, we don't want to hear it. No excuses! Be like Radu and get it done!

For more wisdom from, Radu visit him on Quora:
https://www.quora.com/profile/Radu-Tomuleasa

ARPIT SHARMA

Arpit Sharma, like many of us, has often struggled against negativity in his life. When he was a child, his grandfather told him to go to the Hindu temple every single day. As he grew, he continued to visit the temple every morning. If it were closed for some reason or another, he would find an alternative, even visiting Christian churches.

His aim was not to become more religious, but to bathe himself in positive energy. And the energy you find in places of worship is often an intense, holy, otherworldly vibe. Whether it's from the beautiful surroundings, the presence of deity, or the well-wishings and positive vibes imbued from its parishioners, churches, temples, synagogues, and other places of worship are a great place to experience pure positivity.

However, you don't just have to go to a religious building to experience positivity. Others find calm and positivity in natural surroundings. Others still enjoy time with positive people or positive occasions.

For Jeannie, one of her most positive places is in her parents' living room. The positivity fostered there has not been by accident, but it's impossible to engage in negative behavior in their living room, even if they are not even present in the house. All arguments tend to be taken to the street level. Sometimes during especially stressful times, Jeannie will just pop into her parents' living room, even without anyone present in the house, and just sit in silence to soak up the calm atmosphere.

The key to Arpit's success is finding places that bring positivity for him. So if religious buildings don't bring that sense of peace to you, find an alternate place, whether it's a duck park, a library, an art museum, or even the living room of a friend.

For more wisdom from Arpit, check him out on Quora:
https://www.quora.com/profile/Arpit-Sharma-282

BENJAMIN DAVIS

Benjamin Davis suffers from chronic fatigue syndrome and has found that a daily habit has not only made him feel better but also made him more successful in everyday life. Unable to handle stress due to his illness, Davis took up the practice of meditation.

He began with just one minute of meditation before bed each night and built his way up to a maximum of fifteen minutes, adding in some simple breathing exercises as well. Nowadays, he does a minimum of five minutes per day.

Since starting to meditate, Davis has found that he is more relaxed and focused, and better able to handle interactions with people. Meditation isn't as difficult as you might believe, and with such a low time commitment, this is an excellent habit to promote success. If you've started noticing a pattern in this book showing people meditating or praying, good!

We want to allow you many options and inspirations for adding meditation-like habits into your daily life. People have used meditation to help with all sorts of illnesses, mental clarity, stress, and brain strengthening. And that's just to start.

To get more info on Benjamin, visit his Quora profile:
https://www.quora.com/profile/Benjamin-Davis-50

AKRAM KHAN

Akram Khan started his habit after a civil war in his home country of Kyrgyzstan, during the forty-day curfew and quarantine, when he was stuck at his boss's house. His boss gave him the advice to get up at five a.m. every day.

For Akram, waking up at five a.m. was like having a lightbulb go off. In those quiet morning hours, he was able to exercise, meditate, and clear his head. According to Khan, "Those were the days, when I started taking exercise. Sports changed my body and personality as a whole. I've never fallen ill since that day. Early in the morning, the streets are quiet. I could see the dying stars. During jogging, I could listen different birds chirping, which really creates a positive impact over brain."

We know, getting up earlier isn't possible for everyone. But we'd suggest giving it a good try. Turn your phone off, get to bed early, and try waking up a little bit earlier every morning. You may be working against sleep debt, which is a problem for another habit story, so be patient with yourself. It may be that you are a morning person but have trouble dragging yourself out of bed because you're too tired.

Having time awake when others are asleep seem to be a key habit of many creative types, whether it's night or day. Having uninterrupted time to reflect, think, and connect the dots is extremely important. So if you find that you're really not a morning person and that you like the night, if your schedule permits, stay up a little later and enjoy the starlight and the quiet. Unfortunately, if you have kids or a regular nine-to-five job, this may not be possible. Perhaps trying to negotiate with an early-bird spouse for breakfast duty or with your boss for alternate schedules will work.

If you want to learn more about Akram's practices, check out his Quora profile.

https://www.quora.com/profile/Akram-Khan-462

KAY STRINGHAM

After the death of her young son and a subsequent divorce, music teacher and spiritual director Kay Stringham found herself without much of a support group to help her through the dark moments of her life. She joined a new church to find that community. After one service, Kay—normally a shy, reserved woman—approached Debbie, an outgoing psychologist and singer, about being her friend.

"I literally just walked up to her and asked her to be my friend. I was trying not to burst out into tears or run the other direction." It's been 30 years since Kay and Debbie became friends and yet, every single week, the duo can be spotted in the Waffle House at 9 a.m. on Fridays. They enjoy way too many cups of strong coffee and chat for a couple of hours. Everyone in Kay's life knows that Friday mornings are for WAHO and Debbie, and they never plan anything else then.

Similarly, Kay also has met with another friend every Thursday for lunch. Again, everyone knows not to disturb or plan anything during that time. And if those two social appointments weren't enough, every Thursday night, Kay has all of her now-grown children, of whom Jeannie is one, and their children over for dinner. I don't even have to ask if we are having dinner on Thursday night. I just know I need to show up by 6 p.m., or I get a text at 6:01 asking where I am.

While for many, spending so much time and energy on social engagements may seem like a luxury, for Kay, friends and family are the point of life. Research has shown that a strong social network is one of the biggest predictors of physical and mental health. It's even been shown to increase life expectancy. Kay picked up this hint from her own mother, who also had non-negotiable lunch dates with friends. She lived to be 100. The most common regret at the end of life is not spending enough time with friends and family. It's not, "I wish I spent more time meditating," or "I wish I made more money."

However, these social supports can also have professional implications in your life. Through her friends and their encouragement, Kay has embarked on many projects and endeavors that have added immensely to her life satisfaction, whether working with college students or starting a singles ministry at her church, and even marrying Jeannie's father!

If you want to learn more about what Ms. Kay is up to currently, check out her church website, which updates often with new ministries, job titles, or project titles she's jumped into, probably because Ms. Debbie encouraged her to:

https://www.cornerstoneathens.cc/ourteam

MARY BERRY

Famous cookbook author and TV personality Berry is best known around the world for judging *The Great British Baking Show*. While the 80-something-year-old must taste dozens of cakes while judging for the myriad of shows she hosts, she is also known for her slim figure.

Recently asked how she keeps her figure while eating so much, she answered "with moderation." While her career and hobbies keep her baking with loads of sugar and fat, she says, "I only eat a little bit of it, and I think that is the key to it."

This is a key piece of advice for many areas of life, but especially when it comes to food. The first and second bites of food usually taste the best. Mary tends to bake for guests and parties, which keeps her from eating the entire cake. She'll have a small piece or just a bite.

Additionally, to keep her figure slim, she learns to adjust her intake on days or seasons when she will be judging, and therefore tasting a lot of high-calorie treats. She fills her plates full of veggies and consumes broth-based soups for meals when not judging. This way she can eat the cake and stay healthy, full, and trim without sacrificing any one of those.

If you follow Mary's advice, you can have your cake and eat it too! Moderation does require some willpower, but keeping the end goal (or treat) in mind can help you stay on course. If you know you're going out for dinner and want to get the dessert, you can adjust your intake throughout the day by eating a filling broth-based soup for lunch, or skipping the appetizer.

DAVID ZINCZENKO

David Zinczenko, author and diet guru, had no idea that when he wrote the first column in *Men's Health* called *Eat This, Not That*, it would spawn a massive empire. David's premise was simple: instead of one common food, you could make a small swap for another similar common food, a process that could be stacked for big lifestyle changes.

By making sensible swaps, such as a McDonald's Filet-O-Fish for the Burger King Big Fish Sandwich, you can still eat all the things you want, but make massive cuts in calories, fat, sodium, or processing. Switching to a McDonald's sandwich seems like a funny health strategy, but if you're going to eat that greasy, fried fish sandwich anyway, you'll save 260 calories, 14 grams of fat, and almost 1,000 mg of sodium.

The *Eat This, Not That* empire has spawned TV specials, over a dozen books, a magazine, and a website. It's all devoted to simple swaps you can make and learning to read labels and ingredients to be able to make your own swaps.

Beyond food, the idea of simple swaps can be used in almost every facet of your life. If you're a soap opera junky, switch to drama or romance novels, which at least have you reading. Can't get enough Netflix and chill? Swap out your normal binge of adult animations for informative documentaries. Want to make a change that will help the environment, but still keep your house clean with familiar products? Swap them out for the same brand, but with the concentrate, which uses less plastic.

By getting in the habit of asking yourself what small swap you can make for everything you do, you can build up enough to make a massive change.

To find out all about David and his swaps, visit his website: **http://eatthis.com**

ROBERT MAURER

Robert Maurer, Ph.D., author of *One Small Step Can Change Your Life,* is a psychologist who studies habit change, and a professor at UCLA. Maurer has spent decades studying people and the best ways to build *and* sustain habits that promote excellence and well-being. He's appeared on numerous TV specials, written dozens of books and research papers, and been involved with numerous clinical studies on sustaining good habits. If you want to know how science says to sustain a healthy habit, he's the guy to go to.

According to Dr. Maurer, the best way to make changes is to start out small. He follows the Japanese principle of *kaizen* to achieve results. Dr. Maurer would have approved of Michal's one push-up habit, as he's actually prescribed similar approaches to his own patients, because it's what his research has proven over and over. One patient, a busy and overweight single mother who was at serious risk for heart disease and diabetes, had been told by a previous doctor to exercise at least three times per week for thirty minutes. It never happened. Maurer had her simply walk in place during the commercials of a show she watched at night. That was it. Before long, the mother was doing more exercise than even the first doctor had mandated. Why?

Because she started small. Like with the small swaps suggested by David Zinczenko, small comfortable changes work with the way our brains work. Our brains, generally, dislike massive changes, seeing them as a threat and overwhelming us. But starting out with small changes tricks our brains into being able to make bigger changes.

What small changes can you make to kick-start your big

goals? Think really small. If your big goal is to write a book, simply tell yourself that you need to sit down and open a word processor every day at a certain time. No need to even write anything. If you want to wake up at five a.m., set a silent alarm every night before you go to bed – even if it doesn't wake you up, your brain will start to recognize the signal after setting it every night. Or get up just five minutes earlier every day.

If you want to read more about the concept of kaizen or learn more about Dr. Maurer's research, buy the book on Amazon:

https://www.amazon.com/Small-Step-Change-Your-Life-ebook/dp/B00GU2RHCG/

or visit his website: *http://scienceofexcellence.com/*

DAVID ALLEN

Author, productivity guru, and businessman David Allen is one of the more recognizable names in habit formation and productivity, but it's his system, and even more so one specific rule, that anyone in the world can recognize. And that's the two-minute rule. As Michal and I were collecting stories, one of the most-often-mentioned habits outside of the keystones was the two-minute rule. In fact, it was Allen's book *Getting Things Done* that propelled Michal to start his own journey.

While the two-minute rule—if you can do it in two minutes or less, do it now—seems to have caught on, this is far from Allen's only contribution to small habits that make a big change. After hearing about Allen for quite some time, I decided to read the updated version of his seminal work *Getting Things Done*. While I enjoy the two-minute rule, I find that most of my tasks are far more time-consuming than something that can be done in two minutes.

The small habit that really seems to be the basis of Allen's system has nothing to do with the two-minute rule. It all has to do with writing down everything that you need to do, getting it out of your head. This needs to happen even before the two-minute rule comes into play. The key for Allen is not using your own mind as a filing system, but instead using an actual filing system. Your brain cannot keep track of all the things that you need to do. Once all your tasks, thoughts, plans, projects, etc. are out of your head and on paper (or virtual paper), you can then file them, make projects with sub-lists, do them right away if it takes less than two minutes, or any of a number of other ways you feel necessary.

Allen wants you to write EVERYTHING down, whether it be a work meeting, taking your kid out for ice cream, watching a documentary someone recommended, buying a new jacket for winter, or a random business idea.

I can say that writing everything down has been one of the most helpful tricks I have ever learned. I cannot possibly remember or do everything that comes across my desk. This simple habit has helped me with prioritizing, productivity, and best of all, has tremendously reduced my stress. Writing things down, and then taking time daily or weekly to sort and file these things, has opened up so many opportunities for me and allowed me to clear my mind of the clutter I have lying around.

Michal and Jeannie both highly recommend buying Getting Things Done or visiting Allen's website:

http://gettingthingsdone.com

AARON WEBBER

Aaron Webber, chairman of Webber Investments, attributes his success to one key habit: that of planning.

Planning your day the night before means that you don't wake up to an empty schedule, allowing you to better utilize your time and to be productive. Each evening he prioritizes a handful of tasks that he wants to accomplish the following day, which lets him focus on those tasks without distraction the next morning. And every Sunday he plans what his priorities are going to be for that week, giving him the framework for his nightly planning sessions.

Good planning, as Webber knows, is key to success. Knowing what you're doing and why you're doing it helps decrease distractions and keeps you on task! Whether you decide to make your plan the night before like Aaron, weekly like others in this book, or even in the morning, getting an idea of your day or week is essential.

If you want to learn more about Aaron and his venture capital projects, check out his company page:
http://madisonwall.co/#about

TODD BRISON

Blogger Todd Brison has deliberately fostered a habit that has gotten a lot of flak over…well, the entirety of human existence. It's also one Jeannie does frequently and gets made fun of for. It's talking to yourself.

While talking aloud to yourself is often, and erroneously, attributed to mental illness, it's a great habit to foster, especially for those who have creative jobs or ones that require brainstorming. Talking to yourself can help you in a multitude of ways.

According to Ethan Cross, a psychology professor, in the *New York Times*, "Language provides us with this tool [of talking to yourself] to gain distance from our own experiences when we're reflecting on our lives. And that's really why it's useful." If you want to learn more about the benefits of talking to yourself, you can read the full article here.

Beyond talking to yourself aloud, if that's too weird for you, research shows that other options, such as talking to yourself internally, or through writing, can be just as helpful. Some people talk to their pets, loved ones who have passed on, God, or even inanimate objects (Tom Hanks and his volleyball?). The point is to get some distance from yourself and add some objectivity.

Jeannie and Brison are hardly the only people to deliberately make it a habit to talk to themselves. From movies to presidents, people have been talking to themselves in one form or another since…well, the dawn of human existence.

Want to see how talking to himself has helped Brison? Visit his blog: **www.toddbrison.com**

PHIL ADAIR

Phil Adair is an Australian AdWords expert and digital marketer. He attributes his productivity to limiting his availability, particularly on the phone. He suggests putting your phone on silent when you're working. If you can eliminate the disruption of email, social media, and phone calls, then you will double your productivity.

While we know it's sometimes impossible to make yourself completely unavailable, particularly if you're a working parent, there are options to severely limit your phone disruptions. Put your phone on night mode, but have important numbers granted permission to call through, like a parent, significant other, child, or your child's teacher.

It's not just the calls that can limit your productivity; that never-ending series of notifications from email, work apps, and personal apps can keep you busy nonstop. And let's not confuse busy with productive. If your phone is in night mode, those notifications won't distract you. But, beyond that, think about what apps you're giving permission to alert you. Do you really need to know every time Carol from work emails you about her sick puppy?

To get in touch with Phil or learn more about his AdWords speciality, visit his website on ***http://www.hotclicks.com.au/.***

HENRY FORD

The inventor of the modern assembly line, who was also responsible for bringing affordable cars to the general public, attained his goals by adopting a lifestyle of lifelong learning.

He said, "Anyone who stops learning is old, whether at twenty or eighty. Anyone who keeps learning stays young. The greatest thing in life is to keep your mind young."

Picking books to read is a great place to start, but in our digital information age, education is always at our fingertips. From free resources like Khan Academy and fun apps like Curiosity or Daily Art to high-price designer courses and Mastermind groups, being able to learn from legends in your field or in interests is never hard to come by.

If you are up for it, getting an advanced degree or special certifications has never been easier or more customizable. Many online schools offer rolling enrollment, flexible schedules, and reduced tuition or scholarships.

In today's world, keeping your mind sharp and always updating your skills is a must. With the rate of information entering public consciousness, you can easily become obsolete if you're not learning. While Henry Ford may not have had to deal with Dr. Google, his success was tightly wound into the idea of continuing to learn and implementing those ideas in novel ways. Be like Ford; be a learner.

If you want to start your habit of learning by learning more about Ford and his contributions to society, visit the Detroit Historical Society:

https://detroithistorical.org/learn/encyclopedia-of-detroit/ford-henry

NEIL PATEL

Want to increase your productivity in one easy step? Try the easy habit that Neil Patel suggests: sleep.

According to research, the average American gets an average of 2 hours of sleep less per night than they did 100 years ago. But, according to Patel, sleep is only the start. More than ever before, Americans are working longer and longer hours. Americans take less sleep days, vacation, and time off than any other country in the world. But if you think just because you're not an American this trend doesn't affect you, think again. With our ever-on world, everyone is feeling the pinch.

While getting adequate nightly sleep, which is typically between 7–9 hours per night for the average adult, is a start, Patel advocates the ideal trifecta of sleep, rest, and recovery. It's not enough to just sleep. Taking time to rest, enjoy your day, and spend time talking with friends or family is essential. Additionally, extra recovery time such as vacations or weekends off is needed in order to have peak performance.

In his blog, Patel says, "The more rested your brain is, the more it can do for you during those hours you are awake at work."

Working 24/7, or even 16/7, 365 days a year will not make you more productive. It will make you less. Make it a habit to take time for yourself, your hobbies and non-work-related interests, and your family and friends. Your work and productivity will thank you.

Patel is a famed SEO expert and blogger at www.Neilpatel.com

MARK CUBAN

Mark Cuban, billionaire tech entrepreneur from ABC's "Shark Tank," is an avid reader: He reads everything and claims that he aims for three hours of reading a day. For Cuban, reading is one of the best ways to stay mentally sharp.

While not all of us may have time or inclination to read for three hours every day, extensive reading and lifelong learning are traits shared across all successful people in all areas. "Lifelong learning is probably the greatest skill," Cuban says on Arianna Huffington's The Thrive Global Podcast.

While many of us read articles and shares on social media, we don't often sit down and read entire books. For example, Michal started his journey when he read a *book*. Not a listicle. Not a blog post. A book.

You can start your own journey of reading by picking well-written or critically acclaimed novels, and nonfiction books that pique your interest. If your budget is tight, local libraries are a great place to check out free books. Find a friend who's an avid reader, and borrow from them. Or start on your bookcase. Most people have a few unread books lying around the house.

Set a small goal for yourself, such as one book a month, choosing easier-to-digest literary materials. Don't feel you have to go out and buy *Moby Dick* and read it in a month. The point is to make reading books a regular habit.

And if you are so crunched for time that even reading one book seems overwhelming, start out even smaller to get yourself used to it. Try apps like Blinkist that summarize well-written books into a short chapter. You can do this with a book to see if you'd like to read more of it, or to give yourself quick information on a topic you might not otherwise have known much about. Of course, the goal here is for you to read full-length books too. So don't just cheat and read the CliffsNotes.

E. B. WHITE

E. B. White, author of *Charlotte's Web*, famously said, "A writer who waits for ideal conditions under which to work will die without putting a word on paper." That applies to us all, whatever your occupation is.

In his book review *Writers at Work* he summarizes his own habit of avoidance and how he worked with it:

The thought of writing hangs over our mind like an ugly cloud, making us apprehensive and depressed, as before a summer storm, so that we begin the day by subsiding after breakfast, or by going away, often to seedy and inconclusive destinations: the nearest zoo, or a branch post office to buy a few stamped envelopes. Our professional life has been a long shameless exercise in avoidance. Our home is designed for the maximum of interruption, our office is the place where we never are. … Yet the record is there. Not even lying down and closing the blinds stops us from writing; not even our family, and our preoccupation with same, stops us.

While it's important to have a place you feel comfortable writing or working, whatever your job may be, it's even more important to realize that whether you write/work or not is up to you. Oftentimes Jeannie found herself taking her laptop into the bathroom and locking the door to keep the kids from bothering her while she wrote this book!

To learn more about White, his books, and his contributions to literature, visit his publisher:

https://www.harpercollins.com/author/cr-100460/e-b-white/

TIM FERRISS

Timothy Ferriss, author of *The 4-Hour Workweek*, is famous for many habits. But the one that stands out most, and has the ability to benefit most people, is batching emails.

According to *Forbes*, the average employee spends 2.5 hours a day reading and replying to emails, which is mostly unproductive time, time you could have spent creating or doing high-quality work.

With our ever-present smartphones and their constant notifications, it's very tempting to check our email dozens of times a day. While it may seem like sending off that email quick doesn't add much time to your day, those 5 minutes add up.

To see how much time you are actually spending on email, download an app that can track your time on different applications. Once you have an accurate idea of how much time you're spending, turn off your notifications. It's okay! We promise it won't be as hard as you think.

Ferriss suggests working toward checking just twice a day. He gives lots of tips on how to go about this, including knowing when your peak hours are and setting up an auto-responder with another contact form for emergencies. According to business etiquette, email is not meant for immediate response, allowing 24 to 48 hours for response times. We have to quit training people to expect us to respond immediately on a platform not meant for it.

Visit Tim's blog to learn more about him: ***https://tim.blog/***

Mark Zuckerberg

Among the most successful people in the world, you see the practice of philanthropy: giving of time, money, and knowledge. Facebook founder and CEO Mark Zuckerberg is a great example of the habit of giving.

With an estimated wealth of $71 billion, it's no wonder that Zuckerberg has donated hundreds of millions of dollars to various non-profits and charitable organizations. In 2010, he signed the Giving Pledge, with other ultra-wealthy individuals like Bill Gates and Warren Buffet, where Zuckerberg and his company agreed to give away 99% of the Facebook stock worth over their lifetime.

While he has made it a habit to give large sums of money away every year, he also manages to get involved on a personal level: working with law enforcement agencies to help them manage and take advantage of social media, planting gardens in Texas, and speaking with low-income high school students, just to name a few.

Finding a place to plug in and volunteer can be done easily. Every town has a school that needs mentors. The American Red Cross has chapters in every area. Some positions require some time commitment, while others can be accomplished once in a while. Sign up for a soup kitchen a couple of times a year or go read books to pre-K students so their teacher can get a much-needed bathroom break.

If you have the financial resources, consider giving monetarily, but don't just stop there. Follow the example of Zuckerberg and get your hands dirty too. Once you get in the habit of giving back, it's one you won't want to stop. Giving back to your community not only helps the people in it, but also have been shown to greatly benefit you with increases in happiness and a sense of belonging.

*Find out more about his giving by going to the Giving Pledge website: **https://givingpledge.org/***

JERRY SEINFELD

Tracking habits, in and of itself, can also be a good habit to breed. The habit of tracking can make it easier for us to keep up with certain habits we want to ingrain, or even break.

Comedian Jerry Seinfeld is credited with the red X habit-tracking hack. Every day you do the habit you want to encourage, or don't do a habit you're trying to discourage, you mark it on your calendar with a giant red X. Once you get a nice chain of red Xs going, it's easier to keep it going. No one wants to have a missed X glaring at them from their calendar every day.

If the red X method doesn't speak to you, there are plenty of other options. And we also realize that not every habit does well being tracked. And tracking isn't necessarily related to checking things off.

Sometimes, just an app that keeps track of how much time you spend on social media can help you cut down on it. Research has shown that simply tracking what you eat, without even consciously changing your eating habits, can help you lose weight.

So whether you're going to track your streak with a red X like Seinfeld, or go a more high-tech route, tracking your habits can help you ingrain those habits and keep them up.

Visit Jerry at his website to find out more:
http://www.jerryseinfeld.com

THE MARINES

While the Marines may not be a single person, they have had the same habits so ingrained, they act as a single entity. So when we are looking at habits, there's not a better place to start than with "The few, the proud, the Marines."

We've probably all heard the boot-camp horror stories, from any branch of the military, but aside from special forces, like Rangers or SEALs, the Marine boot camp usually has the worst, or best, reputation, depending on how you look at it. Boot camp is all about instilling the same habits among every last recruit. If you make it out of boot camp, you have some automatic habits that will stay with you until you die. Many of these habits seem trite when you first look at them. For instance, the posture.

Have you ever seen a Marine slouch?

Like making your bed, or keeping your sink clean before you go to bed, posture can be a cornerstone habit that helps other habits flourish. Good posture can help you learn to be aware of your body, which in turn can lead to other habits, like good grooming — which, as we see with the Marines, has cascading effects.

And not to mention, good posture can help keep the chiropractor at bay.

Want to learn more about the habits that Marines foster? Check out the official Marines website: ***www.marines.com***

ALISSA CHEHAB

Alissa struggled for years with getting up and going in the morning. She would get up, take care of a couple of things that were on a schedule, and then would always go back to bed and take a nap. In order to overcome this, she started the habit of making her bed every morning before she got going. This did a couple of things for her: first, it got her up and moving and her blood flowing so she would feel more energized. Second, once her bed was made, she had no desire to get back into bed because it was pristine and neat, and if she got back into bed then she would have to make it once again.

Once she got in the habit of making her bed daily, she found that she started waking up refreshed and ready to take on the day!

Brian Tracy

Brian Tracy is a famous author on the subject of habits, but his most famous book is about his favorite subject: *Eating That Frog*.

Simply put, eating the frog is doing your most difficult or most important task first. For many people, procrastination is the biggest enemy. Emails, pointless meetings, checking social media, and endless little tasks eat up most of their days. You use up all your decision-making reservoir and energy on the things that make little difference on moving you forward on your biggest projects.

In his blog, Tracy says, "All success in life comes from project completion, and living a life of good habits will help you complete more projects."

To eat the frog, first you have to decide what your most impactful project, habit, chore, or activity is, and then schedule time at the beginning of your day to get that done. For me (Jeannie), my frog is writing. After my 30-minute morning work routine of setting my daily schedule, quick check of client emails, and getting my second cup of coffee, I set my timer for 30 minutes and work on personal writing. Whether I'm writing blog posts, my next novel, or even this book, I turn off all my notifications and block out all external demands. Sometimes I go longer than 30 minutes because I get in the zone.

While eating your frog first can help certain people, others require a few quick wins at first to get them feeling productive. If you're going to follow this routine, make sure you set a limit on your small victories and get to your frog as soon as possible. I need the quick wins of making my to-do list and responding to clients in order to put my head into writing.

Other habits that you want to work on, though, work best if you do them first thing. Especially if that habit will give you energy for the rest of the day. Habits like exercise, meditation, or eating a healthy breakfast are ideally done as soon as your feet hit the floor. Lay your exercise clothes out in the morning, and put them on before you do anything else. Going for a 30-minute walk in the morning will wake you up, give you energy for the rest of the day, and give you a feeling of accomplishment.

What's your frog? And how can you make it an early priority?

There's no better way to learn about your frogs than to buy Tracy's book on Amazon:

https://www.amazon.com/dp/162656941X/

ZIG ZIGLAR

Zig Ziglar is a Renaissance man who attributes much of his success to all of his habits. Most of his habits come down to keeping up his motivation. He once said, "Of course motivation is not permanent. But then, neither is bathing; but it is something you should do on a regular basis."

So true for many things in life. It's not like you can hit a light switch and then you are changed for life. The most meaningful and important things tend to need continued effort.

Now, if you want to start your day with getting your motivation up, here are two quick tips from Ziglar:

▪ **Spend 3 minutes remembering your successes.** If you lose your motivation or it is low in the morning, then it is easy to get stuck in looking at your failures and so you get stuck in inaction. So instead, sit down for three minutes and just remember your successes. Let them wash over you and refuel your inspiration and motivation. Some people like to keep journals or bullet lists to keep track of their wins and review them during their morning routines or when they are feeling low.

▪ **Make a list of upsides.** Take a few minutes to write down all the benefits you will get from achieving something, like getting into better shape or making more money. And be sure to include very personal reasons and benefits. Like being able to travel to your dream destination or spend more quality time with your son or daughter. Put that list some-where you will see it every day until you reach your dream.

You can find out more about Ziglar's books and other habits on his website, which has been maintained by his family and

workmates, another notch in his legacy of habits and motivations:
https://www.ziglar.com

BARBARA FREDRICKSON

While I (Jeannie) come from a notoriously hot, sunny climate in the southeast USA, spending time with the Dutch in rainy, damp, and chilly Netherlands has taught me a few things about the need for sunshine and time in nature. I've always taken it for granted. As soon as the sun comes out, every Dutch person is in their back yard. Preparing dinner? Peel the potatoes on the porch.

Spending time in nature whenever possible is a habit that should be cultivated. In our modern world, getting outside is something that needs to be planned. Otherwise, we tend to sit in front of the TV on lovely, sunny days.

Barbara Fredrickson gives some great advice in her book *Positivity*:

"When the weather is good, you need to be ready. Locate a dozen places you can get to in a matter of minutes that will connect you to green or blue, to trees, water, or sky. These have been shown to boost positivity. Perhaps a few natural spots bloom just steps from your door. If so, explore them thoroughly. Make them your own."

Besides being the best source of vitamin D, which increases happiness, sunshine can increase productivity, feelings of well-being, and creativity. Going for a brief walk outside can get your juices flowing, and hiking in wooded areas is about the best natural medication for depression known to man.

So take a page from Frederickson and have spots outside in nature preplanned where you can reenergize your body, spirit, and mind. Maybe it's just your balcony with some pretty potted plants, or (if you're lucky, like me) a giant yard that needs me to get my hands dirty.

Pick a spot, bask in the sun, stick your hands in the dirt, and smell the plants.

Frederickson is a psychologist, professor, and expert on happiness. Visit her blog to learn more ways that habits can increase your happiness:

https://www.pursuit-of-happiness.org/history-of-happiness/barb-fredrickson/

RICHARD WISEMAN

Richard Wiseman is a famous psychotherapist, who wrote the book *59 Seconds*. In it he writes, "In terms of short- and long-term happiness, buying experiences made people feel better than buying products."

The consumerist culture we live in constantly tells us that all we need to be happy is to buy that one more thing. While purchasing products can make us happier, that happiness is not long-lasting. The habit of buying is one that most of us have grown up with, and requires quite a bit of training to reform.

You can start small retraining your buying habit. For instance, instead of buying your significant other flowers for their birthday, you can instead take them out for dinner. You can do this type of swap for even big things: Instead of a fancy engagement ring, go on a nicer honeymoon.

Sometimes when we buy a product, it can also be an experience. So, if you want to buy a thing, buy a thing that can also be an experience. Just don't go overboard or use that as an excuse. Some of Jeannie's family's most-used possessions are board games. On a larger scale, buying a house could be an investment in experiences as well, if you plan on using your house as a place to host family and friends or hold neighborhood parties. Jeannie bought her house so she could have the experience of hosting high school foreign exchange students.

The first thing you need to do in retraining your buying habits is think, "Do I really need this?" and then secondly, "Is this something I can experience?" and then thirdly, "If it's not something I can experience, is there another purchase similar to this that is an experience?" So instead of buying that new bedroom set, get supplies to refinish the one you already have.

Finally, ask yourself why you are buying something. Are you buying that new Apple Watch to fit in? Or because you like new gadgets? Because you're bored?

When you get down to your reason, see what else can fulfill that need. Of course, if you actually do need something, buy it!

To find Richard's books, to book him for speaking engagements, or read more about his current projects, follow this link:

https://richardwiseman.wordpress.com

DAVE ASPREY

Dave Asprey, the founder of the Bulletproof movement, known mostly for its high-fat butter coffee, has plenty of advice when it comes to habits. But rising early in the morning is not one of them. He simply wants you to know your chronotype.

Your chronotype is when you naturally are productive. Most of us already know if we're a morning or night person. According to research done by Dr. Breus, a sleep specialist, there are four types of chronotypes: Deer, or day people; Lions, or early morning people; Wolves, or night people; and Dolphins, or natural insomniacs.

Most western cultures are prone to favor the early morning or even natural insomniacs. School starts early; most jobs want you in between 8 a.m. and 9 a.m. So if you are not a morning person, then you may be at a disadvantage. However, the tide is beginning to turn. With more flexible schedules, work-from-home options, and the gig economy, we are increasingly able to set our own schedules.

As a final note, on making sure you get *enough* sleep, don't assume just because you have learned to do without sleep, doesn't mean your body is really okay with it. Knowing your chronotype should help you get *more* sleep, not be an excuse for why you are chronically sleep deprived. Natural insomniacs are extremely rare, maybe only 1–2% of the population.

For more information on your chronotype, read this post:
https://www.bulletproof.com/sleep/sleep-hacks/sleep-chronotype-circadian-rhythm/

Deborah Natelson

Tea: check. Breakfast: check. Notebook: check. It's six o'clock in the morning, and Deborah, an incorrigible morning person, is ready to work on her novel.

She's also ready to be distracted. Soon, the other people in the apartment will be waking up, neighbors will be getting in their cars, and the children across the street will be playing and running and screaming until the school bus arrives. The curtains are open—she must have daylight—and so the sound comes right in.

"If I hear something interesting, I'll start thinking about it."

So she doesn't let herself hear anything. She gets out her MP3 player. It's more than a decade old and only holds one gig of music—so she's not distracted by choosing what to listen to. More importantly, it doesn't connect to the internet.

Earbuds in her ears, she bends her head to write. The world closes around her: she sees nothing but the page before her; she hears nothing but the strains of music she's listened to dozens of times before, music she now associates with writing.

She can still be distracted, though, until she starts to write. So she puts pen to page and lets her imagination take hold.

*Deborah is the author of over a dozen books and CEO at Thinklings Books, LLC, a speculative-fiction publishing company. You can visit their site at **www.thinklingsbooks.com***

ALBERT EINSTEIN

While some of Einstein's habits we now know were not linked to his genius, and may in fact have been to his detriment, such as smoking, he did have many stellar habits that most certainly contributed to his genius.

In addition to daily long walks and naps, he also committed time to daydreaming, or staring at the ceiling. Most of his grand ideas or breakthroughs came during times when he was not actively focusing on the problem, like when he was staring at the ceiling, sleeping, or walking.

The point of Einstein's helpful habits was to get his brain off the problem and working in a different way. While Einstein liked to walk or stare at the ceiling, maybe you can find something else that works for you. Perhaps washing the dishes by hand, gardening, or looking out your office window. The objective here is to give your brain a break from the job at hand and allow other parts of the brain to tackle the issue.

If you want to learn more about the habits or life of Einstein, check out this quick article:

https://www.lifehack.org/596802/10-learing-habits-that-make-einstein-the-smartest-person-in-the-world

SARAH AWA

People who live with a chronic illness, like Sarah does, generally have quite a bit less energy than healthy people do. But a lot of them still have about the same amount of work per day as healthy people do, so they have to find ways to conserve energy and be as productive as they can be with their lower stamina.

Here are Sarah's daily habits to make the most of her energy and boost morale:

1. **Take care of your body**. Get plenty of sleep, avoid caffeine, and eat healthily. Never skip breakfast, the most important meal of the day. Sarah frequently eats (unbuttered) eggs in the morning, and oatmeal with honey or pure maple syrup, not refined sugar. The key to a healthy diet, in her opinion, is limiting sugar intake and eating pure (not processed) foods—the fewer ingredients, the better. She recommends researching an anti-inflammatory diet, since inflammation underlies many chronic conditions.

2. **Stimulate your brain**. Treating your body well is important, but treating your mind well is crucial too. Maybe your morning shower wakes you up properly, but Sarah's brain needs a bit more of a jump-start than that. She does several different kinds of puzzles while she's eating breakfast, two or three every morning, like a crossword and sometimes Sudoku or Words With Friends. There are tons of free apps to choose from, or buy physical puzzle books to avoid the temptation of phone addiction. Make sure to set a time limit.

3. **Set priorities**. Figure out which task is the most important one of the day. Which one absolutely must get done today? Paying that bill? Writing that proposal letter?

Answering that critical email from your boss? Make a list with a hierarchy; use different colors or a spreadsheet if you want.

4. **Congratulate yourself for your accomplishments**. At the end of the work day, review what you got done and tell yourself you did a great job. Sure, you may have only made it a third of the way down your list, but if you did at least one thing, then you weren't a slacker. (If you're reading this book, you're not a slacker!) You made a small impact on the world. Tell yourself, "I am a hero for doing what I can do." You got out of bed. You tried. You didn't let self-pity keep you down.

Sarah Awa is the author of the book Hunter's Moon from ***www.ThinklingsBooks.com****, and the proofreader for this book.*

GREG MCKEOWN

In his book *Essentialism*, Greg McKeown outlines his plan for what he believes is the most powerful habit that we can cultivate: saying no.

In a world of "yes men," saying no to requests can be a form of powerful yet quiet rebellion. It can be harder for some to say no than others. If you are a natural yes person, then practicing the art of no is even more essential.

McKeown makes is very clear what saying yes to so many things means. We can't actually say yes and do everything. If we pick one thing, we won't be able to do another. Everything in life has a trade-off. And this even applies to good things. If you say yes to feeding the homeless on Tuesday afternoons, which everyone would agree is important, then you are automatically saying no to being at your kid's piano lesson that happens at the same time on Tuesdays.

To be able to know what to say yes to, it's important to keep your eyes on your top priority. According to McKeown, the word "priority" was always in the singular until recent years. You couldn't have more than one priority. Even he admits that it's hard to have only one priority, but he makes a point to keep his priority list low. So when he was writing the book, his family and the book were top priority. Even though he might enjoy feeding the homeless, and they begged him because they were desperate, it would always be a no, because it conflicted with his family priority.

Learn how to get a handle on your top priority and say no to everything else by reading his blog:

https://gregmckeown.com

JAMES CLEAR

James Clear, the author of bestselling book *Atomic Habits*, should be glad just to be alive after an accident in high school nearly destroyed his brain. However, he pushed back, and he credits his full recovery, and later success with his blogging career, to the cultivation of small habits.

But what sets James apart from the rest of the pack is his belief that we create habits based on who we are. If you believe yourself to be a messy person, no matter how many new goals you set or habits you try, you will never be a clean person. Your attempts will always fail.

And James is hardly the first person to say this. You can see this sentiment in literature way back to Solomon, in the Biblical book of Proverbs. "As a man thinketh in his heart, so he is." If you hate exercise, pushing yourself to exercise may work for a while. But if you begin to see yourself as an athlete, or someone who enjoys a particular exercise, then keeping that habit will be easier.

This is not to say you can just decide that you're an Olympic athlete and become one.

James is a proponent of living up to your own potential. For instance, after his injury, he worked hard to become a professional baseball player. While he went on to be a team captain, and earn many other accolades, he never played ball past college. Even though his original dream and goal was never fulfilled, he was still happy with the success he had because he lived fully up to his potential.

Changing your core beliefs about yourself is a hard process. To learn more about James and his ideas on core beliefs, check out his *popular blog at **www.JamesClear.com***

DALAI LAMA

Of all the experts in the world on happiness, an exile with hardly any possessions seems least likely to fit the bill. Yet, the Dalai Lama, and many others like him like Mother Teresa and Mahatma Gandhi, is quite possibly the happiest person alive. And it's all thanks to several mental habits he has cultivated. While meditation may seem like the obvious answer, it's only part of his recipe for happiness.

One particular thought habit stands out the most: his continual choice to believe the best in people. Other research, such as that done by Brené Brown, renowned shame researcher, shows that one of the cornerstones of those who live joyful lives is that of assuming others are doing the best they can, even when it might not be true.

A habit of this magnitude is not an easy one to cultivate. It requires constant vigilance to nip the negative thoughts in the bud before they act like a runaway freight train. It's easy to call the man who cut you off in traffic a jerk. Or assume the person in front of you in line with food stamps is lazy. It's easy to make bad assumptions about others, even when we have learned to excuse our own similar behavior. I'm sure we've all accidentally cut someone off in traffic at least once. But if we stop our thought, and shift it, instead, to letting the person in, or giving them grace, it keeps our stress levels from rising.

You don't have to be perfect at this. You are not the

Dalai Lama. Start small and pick one bias you have against people, and work on conquering that line of thinking. Even if you don't suddenly start being the happiest person on the planet, your blood pressure during the morning commute will thank you.

HARUKI MURAKAMI

Haruki Murakami, one of the most influential Japanese novelists of our day, follows a process of self-mesmerisation while he is working on a project. What is self-mesmerisation, you ask?

For Murakami, it means repeating his routine so often that it mesmerizes him. While on a project, Murakami will never stray from his routine for even a day. He starts writing at 4 a.m. and stops at 10 a.m., and then at noon he goes for a 10K run and listens to music to wind down and refresh his mind. Bedtime is invariably at 9 p.m.

The thinking behind his stalwart routine is this: Your body starts to crave this activity, and it's easier to get in a state of creative flow. Like many other famous people, Murakami understands the concept of decision fatigue. While some like Barack Obama have a personal uniform to reduce decision making, Murakami takes it to the extreme and reduces the decision making of his daily routine to 0.

While most of us don't have the luxury to never vary our routine — hello, children! — we can still follow Murakami's lead by instituting morning or evening routines, or if those times don't work, pick your own best time. Once that routine is in place, follow it every day without fail. That means if you have a morning routine of getting up at 6 a.m. during the week, you still get up at 6 a.m. on weekends.

JOHN MILTON

One of the themes you see running through the lives of creative geniuses, like John Milton, writer of the classic *Paradise Lost*, is that of exercising your brain in the morning and then exercising your body in the afternoon.

Each morning Milton woke up and participated in first his religious habits, and then got working straight away on his writing. Around noon he would stop for lunch, and then he would exercise. Milton is not alone in his routine either. Many other writers, musicians, and artists follow some basic form of this routine: Kafka, Beethoven, Hugo, Darwin, Freud, Strauss.

Contrary to what many of us feel, physical activity helps stimulate the brain, and our bodies tend to hit a slump midday, but exercise can be a great antidote for that. Moral of the story: exercise is a great way to wake up your body and get your mind moving. Even if you aren't the type that likes to exercise first thing in the morning, you can still take advantage of the benefits of physical activity.

Another popular thread among creatives: an afternoon nap.

THE OLD MAN DOWN THE STREET

When Jeannie approached a neighbor, whose peculiar habit always intrigued her, about being in the book, he agreed that the habit could be in, but he'd prefer for his name to remain anonymous.

We don't use the term "old man" lightly here. The old man down the street celebrated his inauguration into the centenarian club two years ago, with so much fanfare that another neighbor had to call the cops.

That's right, he's 102. And he attributes his longevity to his peculiar habit.

Shortly after Jeannie moved into the neighborhood, she noticed an older gentlemen circling the cul-de-sac in front of her house twice, at 1 minute past the hour, from 8 a.m. to 8 p.m. She could set her watch to it.

After noticing this pattern for about a year, she was at her mailbox when she saw him exit his house on the hour, race-walk to the cul-de-sac, and make two laps before returning inside. She repeated her mailbox trip the next day, and walked alongside him as he did his laps.

"We're too sedentary. We need to move more. So I move every hour. Five minutes of exercise."

While 5 minutes every hour doesn't sound like a lot, science actually does support the old man down the street and his 5 minutes of exercise an hour. Frankly, a 102-year-old man race-walking 5 minutes every waking hour of every day seems to support the idea all on its own.

Studies have shown that getting up and walking around a bit every hour is more beneficial than a full 30-minute workout every morning.

Even if you can't find time to fit in a full workout, making sure you get on the move every hour can provide just as much benefit, if not more, than a full workout. If you are exercising for 5 minutes, 12 times a day, that really does add up too. That's about an hour.

So take a break from the computer every hour. Do a couple of push-ups, walk around the building, go up and down a flight of stairs. Just get your movement in and get it in often.

LAURA HERTZ AND ERIK MESSAMORE

Laura Hertz is the CEO of *Gifts for Good*, an e-commerce site that sells premium gifts that support charitable causes around the world. Hertz believes that her most important habit is gratitude. Laura uses a gratitude journal that helps her remember what is important and good in her life.

"First thing when I wake up, I write down three things I have to be grateful for, three things that would make that day great, and one daily affirmation. Right before I go to sleep, I write down three amazing things that happened that day and answer the question: 'How could I have made today better?' The daily practice of writing down what I have to be grateful for, and reflecting upon who I want to become, helps me rewire my brain and improve my happiness."

Science seems to support the idea that the habit of gratitude is a medium for happiness. Psychiatrist, author, and professor Erik Messamore, www.erikmessamore.com, believes so much in the idea of a gratitude journal that he encourages all of his clients with depressive disorders to keep one.

According to Messamore, depression makes you focus on the negative so much that you can't see all the good things in your life. The simple act of writing just one good thing every day starts to rewire your brain to be looking for the positive throughout the day, so that you can write it down at night. The writing down helps to reinforce the positive effects of gratitude. And being able to look back at all the positives that have happened, he is able to help his patients recover from catastrophizing the negatives in their lives.

FRIEDRICH NIETZSCHE

We writers are a strange lot. If you look up strange habits on the internet, most of them belong to creative types, but chiefly writers. Nietzsche had about a million strange habits, but one that is particularly useful for modern people, in all careers, is standing while writing or working. Before the advent of the computer and modern life, much of the work that people did required standing or movement of some kind. But writers would often sit at their desks. He once said in a letter to his writing buddy Flaubert: "There I have caught you, nihilist!" he wrote. "The sedentary life ... is the very sin against the Holy Spirit."

Nietzsche was a famous walker, and later in life he was known for walking great lengths, where he perfected his philosophy.

Nietzsche was hardly the only writer to recommend standing desks, either. Others like Virginia Woolf sang their praises as well. She would set her "easel" up next to that of her sister, who was a painter. Gretchen Rubin in her book on habits, *Better than Before*, talks about her own foray into treadmill desks. And here, you thought these standing desks were some kind of fad.

So, if you can't find the motivation to write at a desk, change your position and get the blood flowing. Try going on a hike and bringing a journal along, or a tape recorder, even your phone, to record your thoughts. Get yourself a standing desk, or even a treadmill desk. You don't have to sprint—just a leisurely stroll can help improve idea flow and motivation.

LISA STEELE

Lisa Steele, author of *Gardening with Chickens* and *Let's Hatch Chicks* and founder of the website Fresh Eggs Daily, makes it a habit to surround herself with positive people. In one interview, she said:

"Social media has become a cesspool for the haters and trolls. Don't let negative people hold you back. Understand that negativity generally comes from unhappy people and those who envy you. Happy, successful people don't tear others down. Surround yourself with ambitious, positive people. It's too easy to focus on the negative and there's just no upside to that."

On the flipside, choosing to also not engage with negative people can be a good first step. Sometimes we can't remove every negative person from our lives, but Steele is right: social media can be extremely negative. So, even if you can only limit your time on social media, it's a positive start. Many of us have intense social media habits.

It's super easy to break that automatic habit if you uninstall these programs from your phone. Really, one click. It's gone. Try it now!

NICK EARL

Nick Earl, CEO at Glu Mobile, a game developer, believes in inverting the traditional workplace hierarchy. To him being CEO means being a servant to the rest of his company, a sentiment shared by the most famous servant leader of all time: Jesus.

In an interview about his success, Earl said, "As CEO, I view my role as making my general managers successful, not the other way around. So, long ago, I decided to check my ego in at the proverbial front door and instead approach my leadership role as one of making divisional leaders as successful as possible."

What a world we could live in if all of our leaders decided to lead like this. Think of the upheaval that Christianity caused, whether you follow it or not, because a quiet carpenter taught his followers that the first shall be last, and lived it, by washing their feet.

The habit of humility and putting other people before you seems very contrary to our current political and business environments, which is why Earl says he inverts the hierarchy.

Brooks Powell, founder and CEO of Thrive+, a supplement designed to alleviate the negative effects of alcohol, like many other successful entrepreneurs, believes in the power of prioritizing. As the CEO of a fast-growing start-up, he's had to learn which tasks are important. Powell's way of dealing with this is renaming his to-do list. He calls it his queue. And he believes in keeping his queue flexible so that more important tasks are allowed to kill off tasks that are unimportant.

"I am always very strict of allowing important things that pop up to be added to the top of my queue so that I get them done first. This means that a lot of things don't get done, but what I have realized is that most of the time if something doesn't become important enough to deal with now, it's probably not worth doing anyways."

There are other ways of rearranging your to-do list as well. For instance, Jeannie's father, an administrative pastor at a large church, has a main to-do list, which includes items like "check your to-dos" and immediately important things, like playing trains with his grandson or ordering supplies for the food bank. If something is unimportant, he moves it to a different list or, if it can be delegated, onto an employee to-do list.

However you decide to do it, make sure you don't get stuck crossing minutiae off your to-do list, or feeling guilty that you never seem to make progress on crossing it all off.

A few tips to use:

1. Make sure the things on your list are things that only you

can do.

2. Keep your most important tasks at the top.

3. Don't be afraid to take tasks off your list without completing them.

STEPHEN COVEY

Stephen Covey is a staple for all. If you have not read *The 7 Habits of Highly Effective People* — you should go do that now — you've most certainly heard about it. While many popular self-help guides promote external habits, Covey leaves the pack and instead promotes internal habits, which he lived by. This emphasis on internal, intrinsic habits is part of the reason his book has remained such a timeless and enduring classic. Since we lack the time and space to go over all 7 habits, we'll focus on just one: Be Proactive.

Simply put? We're in charge of our own lives and how we react. We have a choice, and if we don't choose, then others choose for us. Instead of choosing to be victims of our circumstances, we need to learn to take control.

Famous psychologist and Nazi concentration-camp survivor Viktor Frankl echoes this thought in his seminal book *Man's Search for Meaning*. He encouraged his fellow inmates to take charge of their own meaning. Even in the bleakest place on earth, where there was seemingly no choice for anyone held there, there was still one thing the Nazis could never take: how you responded. And it made all the difference between life and death for many in the concentration camps.

The survivor, proactive mentality of great men like Covey and Frankl is probably the most important habit to have, because without it, all other habits will fail. You will lose out to the victim mentality and your good habits will wash away.

You have the power within you to choose how you will

respond to anything in life, even something as terrible as facing Nazi gas chambers. You have that power, even if your response is to give that power away to others.

DAVID KARP

How often does your alarm go off in the morning, and you immediately pick up your phone and check your social media or email? We've all been guilty of it at some point in time. But David Karp, founder and CEO of Tumblr, has other ideas about email: he checks his email only at 9:30 a.m., never before and never, ever at home.

Why is it so important that we wait to check in?

In a world that's always on, work/life balance has eroded so much that we are always on call. Research has shown that having our brain in work mode all the time can wreak havoc on it. And not to mention the issues that come up with your family.

If you're physically with your family, you should be with them mentally.

With most of us not being able to only check our email at 9:30, here are a few tips to tone it down and be more present.

1. No phone at the dinner table.
2. Put your phone away from your bed so you're not tempted to check your email first thing in the morning, or even in the middle of the night.
3. Schedule an autoresponder for several hours every day where you won't be available, whether it's for bedtime with your kids, dinner with your spouse, or some special alone time.

ANNA WINTOUR

If you don't have your eye on fashion, you may not be aware of the style icon, but that doesn't mean you can't learn a thing or two from her. Most of her morning routine is pretty normal: exercise, breakfast, coffee. Famous people really are like the rest of us!

However, there is one area where Ms. Wintour doesn't skimp, and that's her beauty routine. Every day she has her hair professionally blown out. To many of us, this may seem like an extreme indulgence. However, for Ms. Wintour, it's a sign of her priorities. As the editor-in-chief of *Vogue* magazine, setting trends and styles is her job.

Takeaway: Know your priorities and set habits that fit with it, even if others think it's weird or indulgent. So you're not a fashion maven, and getting your hair done every day isn't right for you, but maybe there's a habit you want to have but it seems overboard or odd. If you're a stay-at-home mother, you might decide you need to get up at 5 a.m. every day and have a no-talking rule while you sit outside until the sun comes up. (Yes, this was a habit of Jeannie's when her husband was deployed and she had a toddler running around yelling 13 hours a day.)

Find your groove. Make your groove a habit.

BALZAC

The afternoon nap. While many creative types enjoy exercising their brain in the morning, and then exercising their body in the afternoon, others like the great thinker Balzac prefer to use their afternoons for a nap. Some, like Darwin, will do both.

After a long morning of exercising your brain, it's important to refuel it. Whether you follow Balzac and siesta or Dickens and go for a walk, give your brain some time off. A nap doesn't need to be long; even 20 minutes can give your brain some time off.

The primary purpose of sleep is to recharge our brain and process information. It's why we start to get more incoherent the longer we go without sleep, and days without sleep can produce psychotic breaks.

During your lunch break, instead of grabbing that tenth cup of coffee for the day and powering through more work, let your brain take a break and find a quiet place to rest. Perhaps there's a break room no one goes to, or a park bench, or even your car. Don't fight the sleep and fatigue that come around after your brain has been hard at work.

CONNECTING THE DOTS

From Michal:
My first habit was a series of push-ups.

Exercise is a keystone habit, one of the very few discovered in research. A keystone habit is like a magical generator for more good habits. A few other keystone habits mentioned online are meditating (or prayer), making your bed, tracking your food, having a morning and night-time routine (which includes getting proper sleep), and eating dinner regularly with your family. I'm sure you noticed that many of the habits in this book fall into one of these categories.

Usually, when you try to develop a new habit it takes a lot of effort. You mobilize your willpower. You create a detailed plan. You follow through ... for a few days. Then you fail and break a streak. You feel like you are starting over. It's discouraging. You mobilize your willpower again, but it's a struggle.

A keystone habit bypasses this struggle. You wake up one day and you realize you not only exercise, but you also started waking up on time, all the time. You have no idea how it happened, but it surely happened. You go back in time, tracking your days, and sure enough, you cannot recall the last time you overslept.

The first additional habit I got thanks to my push-ups was my morning prayer. Well, I prayed before push-ups, but it could be hardly described as a habit. I kept forgetting about my prayers in the morning rush. Spontaneously, I got the idea that I should couple my prayer with my workout.

Both habits solidified almost instantly. I could forget

about my prayer or I could forget about my workout. Forgetting about both was not possible.

For a couple of years, the prayer and consistent exercises were the only benefits from my push-up habit I could put my finger on. But then, after I got one-day time management training in my day job, I was given the book *Getting Things Done* by David Allen.

I wolfed down the book's contents, and despite the fact that I abandoned any attempts on improving my life more than ten years ago, I started implementing what *GTD* preached. My attempts weren't especially successful, but it was the biggest effort to improve my life that I undertook in many years. And I succeeded here and there.

I have to admit: I'm not the sharpest arrow in the quiver. It took me six years to realize that my push-ups were not enough to lose weight. So, one day in 2012 I decided to change my diet. I cut down on white bread. I educated myself further. I eliminated a lot of sweets and introduced vegetables into my meals. And I lost several pounds in five months.

The best thing? It was almost effortless, in the keystone style. I didn't deliberate; I didn't make huge resolutions. I switched white bread for wholegrain bread. I started eating one raw fruit/vegetable per day. I introduced more exercises into my schedule.

And then I read *The Slight Edge* by Jeff Olson. The biggest gift of my push-up habit was that it taught me the value of consistency. In August 2012 I had been doing my push-ups for more than six years. When I heard that:

"Success is a few simple disciplines, practiced every day."

It clicked instantly. I could do well over 120 consecutive

push-ups.

I did 40 per day when I started my habit in 2006. I didn't lose weight, but my strength and stamina increased significantly. This realization brought to my mind other instances when a relatively small habit gave me success.

During summer vacations in high school, I had studied one hour per day, which helped to manage the usual "knowledge gap," which is a result of two months of idleness. I passed the final high school exams with flying colors. I also passed the exams to one of the most prestigious economic universities in Poland.

I was at the bottom of the incoming freshmen class— more than 100 people did better than I on those exams. But in the fourth year I got an education stipend because I was in the top 25% of the students. The habit responsible for that? I attended all the classes. My brighter peers didn't, and it was enough to get better grades than they did.

But those reflections were secondary. The first thing that came to my mind when I read *The Slight Edge* was my push-up habit. I understood the book's message on the downright bodily level. Yes, you cannot do something regularly for a long period of time and NOT improve. It's impossible!

So maybe, just maybe, I could do something else and get better? Could I change my habits and my life?

Why not? If consistent action always bring results, why not start the action today?

Oh, I had over sixteen years of negative conditioning to overcome. It wasn't "today." It took me a month of grappling with the book's message in the back of my mind before I finally wrote down several goals and daily disciplines that were supposed to lead me to achieving those goals.

In the keystone-like manner I started reading and listening to personal development materials. I had been spending a few hours per day with Jim Rohn, Anthony Robbins, Les Brown, Zig Ziglar, Brian Tracy, and other personal development giants—whom we read about in this book. This wasn't a part of any goal or plan.

And I practiced about ten new habits every single day, including speed reading.

After a month, I measured my reading speed. It had almost doubled in thirty days! I was stoked. This initial success glued me to the rest of my daily disciplines where my results weren't so obvious (what can you gain from studying the Bible for ten minutes per day?).

One of the first books I read after starting my personal development program was *The 7 Habits of Highly Effective People*. Prompted by Stephen Covey's advice, I wrote my personal mission statement. In the process of creating my statement, I discovered I wanted to be a writer. The thought was ridiculous, but I noted down in my personal mission statement: "I'm becoming a writer." Mind you, I didn't write "I'm a writer," because it sounded false in my ears. I didn't believe I was a writer. But, possibly, I could become one.

Eight months after starting my daily disciplines, I published my first book on Amazon. Well, a booklet; it is an under-9,000-word-long guide to creating a personal mission statement.

Can you connect the dots now? My push-up habit prepared me to absorb *The Slight Edge*'s message. I decided to turn my life around using small daily disciplines. This decision led me to reading *The 7 Habits of Highly Effective People* and discovering I wanted to be a writer. In May 2013, I published my first book.

How likely was it to anticipate this train of events in 2006? "Highly unlikely" is the understatement of the century.

Not much had changed in my life one year after starting my ten daily habits. I didn't get rich because of my two published books. I wasn't famous. I had the same job and the same family, I attended the same church community, and lived in the same place.

The only tangible changes were in my schedule and in my habits. I stopped playing computer games, reading fiction, and watching TV. I woke up about an hour earlier and did my morning ritual. On a train to or from work, I wrote. I changed my diet and reached my dream weight of 138 lbs. I read twice as fast as I could a year ago.

My daily disciplines kept me going. Eventually, I began to see larger payoffs. Thanks to royalties from my first Amazon bestseller, we were able to contribute to the mortgage and buy a house. I got a few professional certificates and changed jobs (30% salary raise). I became an online life-coach. I started answering questions on Quora.com and got over 8 million views on that platform. I published 16 books (this one is #17). I sold tens of thousands of my books over the past seven years.

I learned how to advertise books on Amazon, and I helped dozens of authors sell thousands of copies of their books.

You cannot connect the dots in advance. When I published my first book, there were no book ads on Amazon. I could not predict that my book advertising service would provide over 30% of our household income in 2019. In fact, I dabbled with the Amazon ads because my sales dwindled to

200 copies per month in July and August 2016.

Habits compound exponentially. At the beginning the growth is slow. The longer you keep them, the faster and bigger the results are.

I still have my push-up habit. I can do 166 consecutive push-ups.

What is more, in the last two years my wife quit her job, I built a new venture from zero to four figures per month, and downsized my day job to ten hours per week. I replaced our day jobs' income with book royalties, coaching, and book marketing fees.

I look forward to the future with anticipation. I feel like I'm doing what I was meant to do. I'm fulfilled.

And this is all because I started a habit of doing push-ups thirteen years ago.

This is how habits work. Developing good habits is the surest way to change your life for better. Embrace this idea.

Act upon it for the years to come. Improve. Progress. Change yourself and change your life.

Godspeed!

INDEX

Women

ABOUT THE AUTHORS

Michal Stawicki—In a few short years, Michal turned from an IT guy (still working quarter-time) into an almost-full-time writer.

He lives in Poland with his wife and three kids.

You can find list of his books on his blog: www.ExpandBeyondYourself.com

For the latest updates on Michal's next book, please visit: http://michalzone.com/

Jeannie Ingraham—Jeannie Ingraham is the Chief Marketing Officer for Thinklings Books, www.ThinklingsBooks.com, and The Literary Consultant at JeannieIngraham.com. In her spare time, she enjoys relearning to bake without gluten, writing fantasy novels about Genies, and watching stupid cat videos with her husband.

A Small Favor

We want to ask a favor of you. If you have found value in this book, please take a moment and share your opinion with the world. Just let us know how it affected you in a positive way. Your reviews help us to positively change the lives of others. Thank you!

CONNECT WITH MICHAL

Thanks for reading all the way to the end. If you made it this far, you must have liked it! I really appreciate having people all over the world take interest in the thoughts, ideas, research, and words that I share in my books. I appreciate it so much that I invite you to visit www.expandbeyondyourself.com, where you can register to receive all of my future releases absolutely free.

Read a manifesto on my blog and if it clicks with you, there is a sign-up form at the bottom of the page, so we can stay connected. Once again, that's www.expandbeyondyourself.com

More Books by Michal Stawicki

You can find more books by Michal at:
http://www.ExpandBeyondYourself.com/about/my-books/

Made in the USA
Middletown, DE
07 January 2020